STUDY HACKS

A Guide to Study Online Effectively

(Techniques and Habits to Learn Better in Less Time)

Helen Chavez

Published By Helen Chavez

Helen Chavez

All Rights Reserved

Study Hacks: A Guide to Study Online Effectively
(Techniques and Habits to Learn Better in Less Time)

ISBN 978-1-77485-412-9

All rights reserved. No part of this guide may be reproduced in any form without permission in writing from the publisher except in the case of brief quotations embodied in critical articles or reviews.

Legal & Disclaimer

The information contained in this book is not designed to replace or take the place of any form of medicine or professional medical advice. The information in this book has been provided for educational and entertainment purposes only.

The information contained in this book has been compiled from sources deemed reliable, and it is accurate to the best of the Author's knowledge; however, the Author cannot guarantee its accuracy and validity and cannot be held liable for any errors or omissions. Changes are periodically made to this book. You must consult your doctor or get professional medical advice before using any of the suggested remedies, techniques, or information in this book.

Upon using the information contained in this book, you agree to hold harmless the Author from and against any damages, costs, and expenses, including any legal fees potentially resulting from the application of any of the information provided by this guide. This disclaimer applies to any damages or injury caused by the use and application, whether directly or indirectly, of any advice or information presented, whether for breach of contract, tort, negligence, personal injury, criminal intent, or under any other cause of action.

You agree to accept all risks of using the information presented inside this book. You need to consult a professional medical practitioner in order to ensure you are both able and healthy enough to participate in this program.

TABLE OF CONTENTS

INTRODUCTION 1

CHAPTER 1: GET ORGANIZED 3

CHAPTER 2: CREATING A STUDY ZONE 9

CHAPTER 3: LEARNING HACKS 12

CHAPTER 4: PREPARING YOUR MIND 18

CHAPTER 5: IGNORING BOTH NON-SUPPORTIVE RESPONSES AND PEOPLE 25

CHAPTER 6: INCREASE YOUR MEMORY 38

CHAPTER 7: STRATEGIES FOR IMPROVING MEMORY 49

CHAPTER 8: MASTERING EXAMS 57

CHAPTER 9: ACTION PLAN TO DEAL PROCRASTINATION . 63

CHAPTER 10: OTHER STUDY TECHNIQUES 76

CHAPTER 11: THE MAGIC OF SPEED READING 95

CHAPTER 12: CHUNKING TECHNIQUE 103

CHAPTER 13: HOW DO ONLINE CLASSES WORK 108

CHAPTER 14: TIME MANAGEMENT TIPS 127

CHAPTER 15: MEMORY AIDS THAT WILL HELP BOOST AND ENHANCE YOUR MEMORY 135

CHAPTER 16: THE QUICK STUDY STRATEGIES 152

CHAPTER 17: PREPARING FOR CLASSES 164

CHAPTER 18: MANAGE YOUR TIME EFFECTIVELY 177

CONCLUSION.. **184**

Introduction

It is said that memory is the brain's ability to store, encode, retain and subsequently remember data or information about our experiences. It is a phenomenon of the mind that allows the organism to remember and store information.

Although we are unique in the sense of human species, often times our memory is affected and does not function as well as it should. The good thing is that there are exercises like mental gymnastics to help improve one's memory.

There are several benefits to having a good memory such as reduced stress levels among other things. Ultimately, a good memory can improve our bodies seeing that the body is an integrated system, we must be mindful of our diet, habits and exercise routines.

In this Book, you will be introduced to strategies that will help improve memory such as the Link Method, Track Method, and Number-Rhyme Method just to name a few. In this Book, you will also find:

- Memorization techniques
- Procedures and strategies to memorize
- Study techniques to memorize, etc...

If you or a loved one is dealing with memory trouble, you are in the right place reading the right book. The methods, procedures, and techniques explained have been rigorously tested and proven by scientists. On that note, take some time and see how much your memory will improve by sticking to the suggestions.

Enjoy!!!

Chapter 1: Get organized

"Work smarter not harder." - Allan F. Mogensen

In 1910 the Ford motor company produced a total of 11 model T's a month. At the time this was an impressive number, but Henry Ford did not feel satisfied. He had a vision and goal of producing a car for the masses and knew he would need to make far more than 11 cars a month. Ford learned that meat packing plants used an assembly line of specialized jobs to effectively package up meats and thought he could apply this strategy to car manufacturing. One year after using the assembly line to build cars, the Ford motor company could now produce a new car every three minutes for less money than when he produced 11 a month. This is an example of working smarter not harder. Henry Ford had a goal, evaluated his current situation, and then came up with a plan to produce the same quality of car at a much faster rate. The phrase "work smarter not harder" is used often these days, but how do you accomplish this? SAT is an acronym to help you remember how to work smarter not harder.

S - Study

A - Adjust

T - Test

Study

The first step in working smarter is to study what your current actions are and ask yourself two questions:

Can I improve what I'm doing?

Can I complete the current task more quickly without decreasing the quality of the product?

The most difficult part of this "study" step is actually taking the time to question what we are doing. Stopping and consciously evaluating your study habits can have a huge benefit. The assembly line allowed the Ford Motor Company to sell 50% of ALL cars sold in the U.S. in 1912.

But if Henry Ford had not evaluated the current way he was building his Model T, he would not have researched the assembly line, changed his manufacturing plants, and altered the history of transportation.

Adjust

Once you have identified a weak area, adjust what you are doing. This step requires some research into the best practices that other people are using. For example, if you waste time each evening searching for school supplies, you can research how others organize their study areas effectively. Henry Ford had heard about an assembly line being used in meat packing plants so he actually traveled to one and studied the assembly line.

Test

After you have studied and adjusted, test your new idea. It has been said that you don't learn from mistakes, but rather from reflecting on mistakes. If you waste time looking for supplies, rearrange your home study area and then see if it actually saves you time. It took Henry Ford several years to perfect his assembly line. He would test and evaluate his new ideas, and evaluate their effectiveness. There is a Japanese term called "Kaizen" which means constant and never ending improvement. These small and constant improvements lead to large improvements and perpetual evolutions in the way we do things. When we play a sport or musical instrument, we improve by testing what we are doing and then making slight adjustments.

I learned how to learn piano as an adult. I would learn a new song by playing it very slowly at first and then try to make one small adjustment. I repeated this over and over and eventually learned the song. Likewise, the many skills needed for school success can be learned by making small improvements over and over again. Eventually, they turn into your habits.

A habit is a routine behavior that is repeated regularly. Some habits you practice lead to success, while other habits can have a negative impact on your life.

Once established, habits impact your life greatly. Take diet and exercise for example. To see the true power of a habit it is best to take a long-term look.

I recently read that the state record for the marathon in South Carolina for my age division (55-60) is two hours and forty-seven minutes. You can't just wake up in your fifties and run a marathon that fast. It takes a lifetime of dedication to exercise and a proper diet. Meanwhile, I have many friends my age that have never valued exercise and therefore cannot even run one lap around the track. Habits are very powerful because they act similar to compound interest. Compound interest has been called "the most powerful force in the world." For instance, let's say you start with $10,000 and add $100 a month. If you make 10% interest, after 5 years you will have $24,000 dollars. Keep up this good habit and after 30 years you will have $391,000. After 40 years you will have over 1 million dollars. Habits can have the same impact on your life. They are the day-to-day choices that accumulate over time to your lifestyle. The goal of this book is to introduce you to many habits of my top students I have observed over the past twenty plus years. By applying some of these good study habits to your life, then over time they can have the same impact that compound interest has on the money.

Summary Points

Improve your grades by applying the habits of top students. Focus on these five areas.

1. Organization

2. Workspace

3. Time Management

4. Study Aids

5. Test taking strategies/Project strategies

Small changes in your study habits can lead to big results.

Analyze your peer group and choose your friends wisely.

Learn to apply SAT: Study, Adjust, and Test

Chapter 2: Creating A Study Zone

Think of your bedroom as your own personal studying sanctuary. Fill it with objects which create study-friendly environment and make sure it is a place that you want to study in. Plants will help to give your room a fresh, natural feel, and objects with bright colors will inspire you (as long as you don't get too distracted).

If you don't have a desk, get one! This is going to be of critical importance to you for the next several year of high school if you want to pass. Instead of buying a desk, consider making one. Milk crates are the best tool for this. They can be found at the back of any cafe or shop (who won't mind if you take a couple, I'm sure) and if you're creative enough can be used for almost anything. With twelve crates you can construct a desk by getting a sheet of wood and stacking three crates beneath each corner of it. In the past I've created a desk, bed frame, bedside table and even clothing shelves from them.

The lighting in your room is extremely important as well. A room with poor lighting can be destructive to your studies as it will leave you feeling unmotivated, tired and even sad. You want to experience the opposite of these emotions any time you go to study.

To achieve these high, positive emotions you can do a number of things. Exercise is a fantastic way to get your mind and body ready to study. A lot of people wrongly assume exercise is bad for study, because it will make you tired. It in fact does the opposite! Spending even a short amount of time running, jumping on the spot or even doing sit-ups and push-ups will elevate your heart-rate, pumping oxygen all around your body. It will release special hormones that elevate your mood and sharpen your mind, putting you in the perfect state for study.

Another way to get pumped up for study is to create a study music playlist. Music can massively increase your concentration levels while studying, as long as you are listening to the right type of music. Anything with lyrics is a no-go. Trying to remember passages of words or tackle difficult topics is made near impossible if someone is singing words into your head. A much better alternative is to find soothing instrumental music to aid your study. This doesn't necessarily have to be classical music, but might be the instrumental versions of a couple of your favorite songs.

Cleanliness is the last thing you should strive for in your studying temple AKA your room! A cluttered room leads to a cluttered mind, and this leads to poor learning. If your room is messy then the priority should always be to clean it up! If you attempt to study amongst the mess you'll find that you either become distracted by the mounds of clothes surrounding you, feeling almost trapped under them, or you will feel guilty that your room is looking so untidy. If you can keep your room pristine and clean, you will be much more enthusiastic about going there to study.

Chapter 3: Learning Hacks

Learning is not just applicable to students because it is confined within the four corners of the classroom. It is a continuous process that can last a lifetime!

If we experience learning everyday either through cooking a new dish, playing an new instrument or switching from windows to mac, it is just proper to learn how to do it in ways that are much easier.

11. Create a cheat sheet (even if you aren't allowed to use it)

Remember in school when you could bring one index card in and write whatever you wanted on that one card to use for the test? Well even if you can't still do that, keep doing it!

The simple act of forcing yourself to put the most important key words, phrases and definitions jam-packed on one small notecard or one double sided piece of paper will force you to get to the heart of the material and cut out all the rest. Since you are ruthlessly cutting out things for space, you are left with the most critical essentials! This will do amazing things for your preparation for the test or exam. Try it.

12. Be Organized

Being organized is needed to increase productivity and lessen down time. You should pay close attention as to how you write your notes, keep your references and store your study supplies.

Immediately knowing where all your things are allows for easy referral and lets you to focus on doing more productive things. Use post-its and to-do lists to help you remember important requirements and deadlines.

13. Use timed Intervals with a Stopwatch. (plus Hydrate)

Get a stopwatch and break up your studying into 7 minute power segments with a one minute break to get up and walk around and stretch in-between. In these 7 minute intervals are like sprinter training their sprints in a very small period of time. During the 7 minutes, go as you can through the material. Harness all your vigor and energies to learning as much as you can on a particular page for example. Then have a minute rest and start the watch again.

By creating the added urgency of the a stopwatch and timing yourself, you will be adding the power of intervals to your study routine and create heightened energy as well!

Also during all your studying, make sure you have plenty of water! Your mind and body is more responsive and is able to process information better when it is properly hydrated.

By simply drinking enough water per day, you are already increasing your chances of improving the overall mental processes of your brain. Take note that you can also snack on fruits that are good sources of water. These include avocado fruit salad, mango-coconut smoothie, or watermelon and strawberry bites.

14. Power Burst of Exercise

Add a quick sprint around the block to you study routine. The added blood flow and endorphin rush will make you look at the material fresh and you will have heightened senses going into studying post-workout. It can be a quick 5 minute run. Anything to get the blood pumping!

15. Youtube It!

To get to the heart of what you are studying, it may help to have a visual perspective. What better way then look whatever you are studying up on Youtube! This is the world's largest video database and contains video content on any specific topic imaginable. You will most likely be able to view short movies, documentaries or news reports on your very subject. It helps bring your material alive and may make the concepts easier to understand.

16. Power through your information double time

Record your voice speaking out the material on a voice recorder on your computer with program like Audacity. Then playback the material to review and listen. You can set the playback speed for your voice to double time so you can review the key information twice as fast!

17. Make use of different materials

Make the best out of your gadgets by not only using them for entertainment but also for educational purposes. It has been found that retention is increased when you get information through multiple media. You are able to recall and retain information when you read or write it down, listen to an audio book, watch video tutorials or documentaries related to the topic.

18. Read upside down.

When you really want to comprehend and pay attention to what you are reading, try this mind-bender! Turn your textbook completely upside down. Now read the sentences from this vantage point. Because it will be much more difficult and challenging, you will be paying attention to every word AND much more likely to retain the information than mindlessly skimming and reading content over.

19. Teach

Teaching a material means that you have a full understanding and mastery of it. Sharing your knowledge to other people is advantageous not only to the listener, but also to you. If you don't have anyone to speak to, get a stuffed animal and speak the material to him/her. Whatever works!

"In learning you will teach, and in teaching you will learn."

— Phil Collins

2o. Reward yourself with snacks

Have you ever found yourself struggling with finishing a required reading assignment? Push yourself to read and comprehend the material by setting a goal and rewarding yourself with a treat whenever you accomplish that goal. For instance, you can eat a piece of chocolate for every 5 paragraphs that you read.

Chapter 4: Preparing Your Mind

Do you currently just study when you need to, or when you feel like it, with the belief that the more hours you put in the better your results should be? If this is the case, then you are very likely failing to get the best return from the hours that you are putting in. Effective studying is not just something you can do as and when you want or need to; you must first be both mentally and physically prepared. Your brain is not like a light bulb which can be switched on and off at random, and will perform at its optimum just because you need to study hard.

The following are some tips and things for you to think about in order for you to be both physically and mentally at your best when engaging in study.

•Determine when you are at your most productive during the day. Some people are adept at getting up very early in the morning and putting in a few hours of hard studying before their daily routine of lectures or work commences. Others struggle to get going in the morning, and cannot function that well so early in the day. Or perhaps you are someone who prefers to stay up late in the evenings, having found that it is the best time for you to put in those extra hours of study and revision. Whichever time of the day suits you best, try to schedule your studies to fit into that timeframe, and also try to get into a steady routine so that it just becomes a natural part of your day. The more disciplined you are, the easier it will be, and the more productive you will become.

•A healthy body leads to a healthy mind, so do not be tempted to sacrifice on your physical exercise in an attempt to gain more time to study. A good walk or a jog in the park will not only benefit you physically, but mentally too. Additionally, it is a great opportunity to reflect on your studies, to think problems through, and to appraise your progress in relative peace and quiet.

- Before you sit down and start studying, make sure that your mind is free from any distractions. Finish any chores that you need to get finished before you commence work. Make any phone calls that you may need to make, check and reply to any emails or text messages that require a response, and so forth. With all of these things completed and out of the way, your mind will now be free of these distractions and not wander off when it should be fully focused on the work at hand.

- Prior to starting your work, you should also make sure that you have eaten and are not going to get hungry while studying. If you are hungry, you will not be able to concentrate properly, and you do not want to interrupt your allotted time by having to go off and get something to eat. While studying is mental work rather than physical work, your brain also needs energy to perform at its best. The brain expends glucose while it is active, so do not skip meals in an attempt to gain extra study time, as this will prove to be counterproductive. Keep yourself hydrated by drinking plenty of water. Moreover, try to eat healthily, rather than just grabbing a snack or other low value convenience food. You may have noticed that many companies have free or subsidized restaurants for their staff where they are encouraged to take lunch. The reason for this is not so much as a perk for the employees; rather it is because research has shown that we are more productive if we eat regular meals and are not hungry. By providing their staff with lunch, companies have noticed an improvement in productivity during the afternoons. That being said, studying after a heavy meal is also not a good idea, as it tends to make us feel lethargic, which is definitely not how we should be feeling if we want to get the best results from our endeavors. Avoid alcohol before and during study time, as it too will make you languid, lacking in concentration, and diminish the effectiveness of your hours of study.

- Make an effort to stay calm, stress and panic free. Anxiety and racing thoughts will be both distracting and use up your brain's valuable energy supply. Instead, endeavor to keep relaxed, think positive rather than negative thoughts, and have self-belief. You have gotten this far in your studies, so there is no reason why, with effort, you should not continue to progress. Think about the possible opportunities that will open up to you by achieving your goals, whether it be getting into college or a university, graduating, or securing a position at a firm that you have been hoping to work for.

- Do not attempt to study when you are tired, as you will not be able to get the best out of your time, nor will you be able to retain the information you are attempting to take in. It is far better that you take a rest before you do start studying, so that your brain is re-energized and fresh. A lack of sleep will also badly influence your brain's performance and ability to process and retain information.

•Take regular breaks during long periods of study; maybe a ten minute break after an hour of study, or a twenty minute break after an hour and a half, whatever you find works best for you. Again, this has been the subject of many studies, and is the reason that you will find that most lessons or lectures are scheduled to last between forty minutes and an hour and a half depending on the age of the students. Longer than that, and the students lose their ability to concentrate and retain information.

•When it comes to exam taking, it is important to be fresh and relaxed before you go in to write. Ideally, you should try to get a good night of sleep the night before. Stop any last minute revision at least one hour before you write the exam. You need that hour to relax, prepare yourself, to eat something, and to allow your brain to rest. If you do not know your work by this time, panicking and trying to brush up on facts at the very last minute will do more harm than good. You will end up being flustered and stressed, which is not the state of mind you need to be in to perform well during the exam. It is also very unlikely that you will retain this information for use in the exam in any case.

Chapter 5: Ignoring both non-supportive responses and people

We believe that we control our mind and our thoughts, but that is a mistake in most cases.

In fact, when we talk about emotional intelligence, we usually focus on a situation of emotional control when we are calm, in a meditative attitude, at rest, or simply when we do not have any kind of problem that we have to solve.

But ... what happens when it is your mind that begins to send messages, thoughts, and emotions in situations of tension, stress, overwhelm, fatigue, or critical moments?

Well, it is not so easy to control our mind and that is when we realize the great influence it can exert on us and how in the vast majority of cases we end up succumbing to it, although we believe that it is not so.

Your mind will try at certain moments to deceive you and persuade you to limit yourself to survive. Understand, that is your job and your function (at least a part of it).

It is adapted to a kind of comfort zone and when you leave it, it feels uncomfortable, so it sends you messages so you can return to the area where it works best. But if you stay in that area, you can never progress. You can never grow, develop, expand, and achieve goals and objectives that are now unattainable for you. And not because you are not qualified for it, but because your mind will do everything possible to make you return to your safety zone in which it is at ease.

If you do not know how to cheat your mind, simply ignore the kind of messages that it tries to make you see. The moment you are that hard with it, you begin to realize your true abilities and that the obstacles are actually the fruit of your own mind.

Always try to find that place in your interior where there is no grief or pity about you. That place where your mind cannot access with its influential messages and in which anything you do; it will be free of conditions of any kind.

Apply this in all aspects of your life; in your work, in your personal relationships, as a couple, in your leisure time, in your sports, in your moments of tranquility. Meditate and find that place in your interior that your mind can not access or control. Maximize that site and rely on it to help you for your purposes. Once you control that small space, you can get everything you want.

Ignore people who hurt us psychologically

Also, sometimes to live we have to ignore many people

To be happy we have to know how to ignore many people. We have to learn to live and to neglect those acts, words or feelings that pretend or manage to annul us.

There are simply people who are conflictive and who torment you with their complaints, their judgments, and their dramas. This can be overwhelming and highly toxic because it conditions your well-being to the uncertainty of their actions.

That is why you have to stop feeding those exchanges that suck your energy and cloud your reality. So the first thing to learn is to ignore certain people in those times when they are hurting you.

Get away from everything that keeps you away from yourself

Stay away from what hurts you, from what darkens your life, from what becomes sinister. Get away from toxic people because your health will appreciate it. Do not let your world crumble.

The emotional balance must be on the side of your well-being and, although suffering is inevitable and you must accept it, it is imperative that you know how to handle it at will. That is, the demons sometimes have to be hugged to see them as less bad.

Do not forget that from time to time we have to discharge. The mind, like the body, must detoxify itself from free radicals, from negative emotions, from conflicting pasts, from people who destabilize it.

Letting go the suffering

Saying goodbye to suffering can be a complicated task but sometimes it is important to stop and re-establish your priorities. That is why you must consider escaping from painful emotions, those that are not healthy and that torment you, that prevent you from evolving.

Remember thatthe things that bother you is not factual issues, they are the way you make of them. This is why it's essential to be able to recognize, communicate and appreciate your feelings in a way that is strategic. Here's a look:

1. Express your feelings and feelings

It is said that sometimes you don't require an enlightened mind to talk to us, but rather a open heart to listen to us. Your emotions are created to be felt, and keeping them in anxiety only makes your life more difficult. If, for instance, you are prone to accumulating sadness, it can make depression appear more apparent.

2. Review the beliefs that support the repressed emotions

It is normal to are worried about how you perform in your studies however, you shouldn't be a disaster if you make mistakes as this can only create negative feelings. This is because there is no greater storm than that which develops in your head.

It's not the same as thinking that it's a tragedy that our son is leaving the house, or to believe that even though it is sad that he's left, it's normal for him to have done it. This can lead to the appearance of depression and anxiety.

It is possible to adapt this logic to various emotions. In this manner we need to be able to fight guilt, but not denial and to get rid of guilt but not remorse. And to rid ourselves of anger however, not in anger.

3. Removing, changing and purifying these emotions and feelings

Examining your feelings and emotions isn't enough. You need to discover what is hiding in them. That is how you can free your mind and body. It's possible that a portion of the crazy remains in your feelings and thoughts however, what needs to know is that you must not allow it to grow.

Don't let go of those who create your beautiful world.

Don't let go of the persons who help make your life beautiful. Let the ones who sabotage it go. Make sure you keep in your life anything that is helpful to you and will make you an improved person.

The pain, the suffering, and the sacrifice of your life will not prove your worth as a human being , nor does it help you improve It only afflicts you and causes you pain. Being surrounded by negativity stifles everything that is shining in you.

Five tips to avoid people that make you feel uncomfortable psychologically

There are some people who because of their behavior or certain beliefs even when they're close, could be prone to imbalance. Is it possible to save the relationship without losing emotional wellbeing?

Through your life, as you grow your circle of friends and make friends, you will form bonds with certain people, despite differences and stressing the coincidences. For others, you might not be able to share the same bond and remain friends or even partners.

What happens when the differences impact your mental health? There are some people whose style of living and their behavior don't match yours, and maintaining a close connection with them could be detrimental to you as their behavior can harm you, hinder you or hinder you from being able to fully understanding the world around you.

There are relationships that, while they provide you with positive aspects when they are put on the scale, they can cause more harm than positive. These are relationships that can ruin your life and can end up creating negative emotions are not what you require. However, most of the time they aren't willing to change their ways, so you have only one option to get to get them out of the way: avoid them, or, rather you can learn to be tolerant of their behavior. It doesn't sound sensible to compromise your mental health to stay in the relationship that's causing harm to you.

1. The negative criticism

They are constructive provided they are based on an objective to be constructive and can help us correct an error or develop. There are some who are only interested in the pleasure of criticism and are causing harm to other people. If we wish to protect our self-esteem, then we should learn to ignore the critiques. When you've identified an individual like that who is only prone to making negative criticisms, do not worry about what he might think about you. In the end, your views won't allow you to grow , and will just serve to weaken you.

2. Ineffective comparisons

Everyone has an inherent instinct to compare. Actually, it's one of the fundamental operations of the mind, due to which we draw inferences. But, there are some who use comparisons to influence us emotionally. People who don't feel satisfied and look at our actions, decisions or actions with other people, to make us appear poor. Naturally, if you are anyone who continually criticizes your accomplishments, it's beneficial to not listen to their views.

3. Unfounded concerns

We often worry however there are those who are truly experts when searching for the reasons to be worried. They are those who aren't happy with every solution, who concentrate on the negatives and always look for disasters or mishaps. Of course, you do not have someone like that to be around in the world. This isn't about having the mindset of a childish optimism that won't get you far, but having people around you that only focus on the negatives could cause depression and discouragement to your progress, and putting you in the state of mind where you only anticipate the most negative outcomes. It is therefore better to be able to ignore these kinds of forecasts.

4. Unnecessary security concerns

The person who is the expert in every aspect: They always have something to say, and they are accountable for minimizing your opinions and making you feel inadequate. They create a profound anxiety, reducing your self-confidence and could make you feel like you are in an emotional blockage that stops you from reaching your goals. So, it is important to avoid these comments and behaviors in particular those who do not possess an in-depth understanding of the circumstances at basis and do not aid in the development of the idea you're considering.

5. The wrong people are to blame

There are those who can see the blinders in the eyes of their peers but aren't in a position to see the light in their own eyes. People who do this often use guilt as a way to control you, making you feel ashamed of yourself to the point where they could make you their slaves, since your decision-making and mind are dependent on their preferences. They are the ones who make promises that they are always satisfied. It is essential to be aware of the attempts to blame you to avoid falling into their gang.

What will you gain when you decide to put aside the negative influences?

If you are able to stop and ignore all of these thoughts and beliefs, you will find that you are able to listen to your inner voice more clearly. You will be able to connect to your most intimate "ME" to figure out the things you truly would like to achieve. If you stop worrying too much about what other people consider your character, you can discover the things you truly enjoy. While doing this you are filled with energy you never knew existed because the people you have been judging sucked up the majority of your mental resources. These are resources which you now can put into yourself, to improve your character and pursue your goals.

Chapter 6: Increase your memory

You are aware of the importance of implementing studying habits and using methods to make learning more efficient and more enjoyable, you are able to begin to explore ways to improve your memory.

It's important to keep in mind that learning what you're taught is more beneficial than getting an exam with straight A's. Do not practice the mindset of trying to study hard in order to be able to be able to pass the test.

Do not study because you're hoping for an A+, but because you are eager to improve your knowledge. This attitude will allow you to see studying as something you can look forward to instead of an obligation you have to meet. Consider your marks as a reward for doing your best to learn something new, and mastering the concept.

"Don't pursue success, chase excellence, and you will be successful"

~ Ranchoddas Shamaldas, Three Idiots

To ensure that you remember all the information you've worked so hard to take in, here are a few tips to improve your memory

21. Pick the most convenient moment to learn

A practical method to make studying simpler is by choosing the time of the day when you are the most awake and alert. This can be beneficial because it reduces time and effort and has been proven to be more enjoyable and productive. There is no one time that is suitable for every person. To help you decide on the most suitable time for you, take a look at these factors:

a. Attentiveness

It is possible to see if are more effective at studying at the beginning of the day or in the evening by experimenting with each of the times and then reviewing the results afterward. It is more likely that you will perform better when you know the moment of the day you will be able to perform most effectively.

b. Interruptions

It is best to pick a time during the day when you are in your home or dorm room in order to avoid distractions. It is essential to figure out a way to stay clear of any distractions during your time of studying as they can be harmful to the success of your studying session.

C. Consistency

You must have a designated period of study which is followed at a minimum of a few days each week. It is essential to stick with it so that you can establish a routine and integrate it into your routine. If you do this every day your body and mind will adjust and become accustomed to being

automatic focus to be alert and focused for particular time.

"Excellence is an art that is acquired through practice and habituation. We do not behave in a manner that is correct due to virtue or excellence, but prefer to have them because we've acted in a proper manner. We are the things we regularly do. Therefore, excellence is not a single act, but a way of life. "~Aristotle

22. Draw diagrams

It is possible to establish connections between concepts simpler by creating diagrams. They are an excellent method of organizing and visualizing concepts and even chemical formulas for quick access and retention.

23. Memorization techniques

Create the concepts you're learning more memorable by coming up with inventive ways to help retain the information more effectively. It is possible to do this using imagination and association. Create a story based on the things you're learning to help you remember them by linking them with positively-colored mental pictures, and exaggerating the significance of them, and adding some humor.

24. Get enough rest and sleep.

Instead of pulling off an all-nighter to memorize every lesson to pass the finals, force yourself to regularly study as well as get adequate time to rest and get enough sleep. Insufficiency of these can not only affect your performance on the exam but make you feel tired and sleepy throughout the day long.

25. Make use of Whiteboards

Learning and studying is enhanced by organizing data visually inside your mind. A whiteboard from your old school can accomplish this! You can pick up a small one for your home office at places like the Container Store (www.containerstore.com) That is where I got mine. It is also possible to utilize your dorm's study area's whiteboard or a blank classroom. Any way to present the information before you in a visually appealing way that can help you connect ideas and help cement your learning for you.

26. Techniques for taking notes

Processing and understanding the information given in class is essential to getting a better understanding of the information. Not able to write down everything your teacher will be difficult, particularly when you're writing and listening simultaneously. It is possible to use tape recorders to be sure that you don't be able to miss important information and to record them as fast as you are able as while the presentation is fresh in your mind. To improve your note-taking abilities take note of these suggestions:

a. Cornell Method

This method involves breaking the page into three parts.

Utilize the ruler to draw a vertical line to the right, and horizontal lines on the bottom, which are approximately 2 inches in length. Utilize the left side to record the major subjects and the most important points and questions. The largest portion in the middle should contain the specifics of bullet points, formulas as well as diagrams or sketches. The last section is designed for you to write your own words on the summaries the notes.

b. Split Page

The method is like the Cornell method, however it's more straightforward. It is all you need to do is divide an entire page by putting an vertical line in the middle. Note the primary ideas on one side, and the second ideas on the other.

C. Do what is best for you.

There is no need to use any other approach than one that you find effective. To determine the best methods that will allow you to be more efficient and faster at learning you must determine your preferred learning style. It is the VARK theory is among the most well-known theories regarding learning styles. VARK is a term used to describe students who learn through audio, visual, Reading or writing and Kinesthetic learning.

a. Visual

The best learning materials for students who are visual include flash cards, videos or charts. Learning becomes easy by using charts and symbols for their notebooks.

B. Auditory

Auditory learners are the best at absorbing information when their teachers are excellent communicators. They also are more likely to remember the information when reading aloud to them or participate in conversations with their peers.

C. Reading

The students who are most successful in learning through writing and reading in text prefer to use textbooks and handouts to study. They also prefer to note notes word-for-word.

d. Kinesthetic

Learners who are tactile or kinesthetic benefit from experiences that are hands-on. They are more likely to learn by moving around, rather than only listening and reading. The learners who are kinematic prefer actions that allow for the practical application of ideas. This could be done by experimenting or by setting up an area that allows all of your sensory senses, keeping your from getting bored easily.

The majority of people are a mixture of these different learning styles. The most important thing is to identify which one you prefer to maximize you learning.

27. Don't Multi-task

It is impossible to complete multiple tasks at the same time. Actually, it can increase the amount of time is required to complete these tasks simultaneously. The act of checking your e-mails, texting or taking notes as you listen to your music do not constitute multi-tasking. You can only shift between tasks but you are not able to give your complete attention to any of them.

28. Meditate

Working memory is responsible for storing the newly acquired information for a short period of time.

Once you've finished the particular piece of data, it's or is transferred to your long-term memory and retrieved in the future, or you lose track of the information. It is typically able to hold up to seven items in the case of an adult.

It can be strengthened and improved by meditative practice. Meditation can help you focus and enhance your memory within a few weeks of practicing. It's also an excellent way to lower anxiety particularly before the examination.

29. Talk the material out loud in your own language.

Get up and make use of your voice. Speak out loud about what you're studying stimulates your entire body as well as your voice. In addition, you're being able to hear (auditory) your voice when you talk. This stimulates your senses. You also must make sense of the content and formulate sentences to express the situation.

It is important to practice reading in the book, but also using paraphrases (where you combine all the information in your own phrases) This is a highly effective method of learning since you're creating the material within your own head and in your own unique way. In essence, it is part of your.

30. You must have the appropriate background music

For me, the high-paced Trance music that is fast and energetic puts me in a state of hypnosis in which I be studying for hours. Certain types of music are similar to other kinds of music. Anything that is powerful enough to get your blood circulation while you learn, but also not distract you from your studies, is great. Beware of music that is distracting with the use of loud voices or shouting. Many people believe that classical music as well as the sounds of nature can improve their moods and aid them to learn better.

Chapter 7: Strategies for Improving Memory

Can you recall the food you had for dinner the day before? What were your clothes? Are you sure you'll be able to pass the driving test again or the test you loved so much? The reason why it takes you time and effort to recall all this lies in the method you employ.

Strategies to speed up your learning and to retain more

Strategy #1: Recite loudly while you read

Sometimes, we attempt to repeat things that we read and then memorize them. We repeat the same thing repeatedly in our minds , but we do not repeat it out loud.

If you're looking to retain the information you've learned You should try listening to it aloud. It's a good idea since while doing this, you're preparing your brain to store the knowledge using images and sound.

What is the significance of it? It is because your thoughts are internalized by your brain, since the thoughts are converted into words. This means it's much easier to recall because your brain will change your thoughts into something that is more authentic.

Strategy #2: Keep a record of everything you wish to remember

If you are able to get an idea of what you're going to learn, particularly when it is explained by a teacher, you can begin recording the segments. There are also applications which allow you to modify various fragments of the recording at any time you require it. In the same way, when you want to create a full song, it would require some effort.

After recording, you can download the recording to your smartphone and play it back when it's time to work. Be sure to read the recordings attentively as you work, so that you can be sure that the information is quickly retained.

The first few times , it might seem a little odd to hear your voice over and over again however, you'll eventually get comfortable with it. Make sure you are critical of your recordings of the agenda , and ensure that they are in written form. The court will review them the same way you do If you think it's boring, uninteresting or unclear You can improve and make it better.

Strategies #3: Record down everything you'll need to keep in mind

Notes on your notes help you identify key concepts such as definitions, terms and formulas. It is possible to write them down on a separate sheet or make flashcards. This will make it easier to remember the key points to be aware of and also use your cards to use wherever you want.

Writing them down can help you use your visual memory. If you've got a strong mental memory for visuals, this method will be very helpful. If your strengths are built on your auditory memory, writing them down will aid you to listen to it and help to reinforce it in your mind when you write.

If you're in a position to do so you have, don't be limited to writing them just once.

It is possible to write notes multiple times in order to remember the information. It might seem like a long task, but if you want to retain the history of your area or general information, it is extremely beneficial. If you're trying to learn formulas it might not be as efficient.

Strategies #4: Repetition of the information and then memorize it

According to a recent study conducted the use of repetition as a method for learning is a natural and efficient method to reveal the mechanisms that the brain employs to store information into the memory. The study examines the neurological effects on the brain that result from the repetition of information that one would like to acquire in working memory[4[4].

Learning is the process of enhancing the strength of particular neural circuits, based on exercises. This repetition isn't identical to that described in the first strategy. It is more of repeating the data stored in memory in order to not forget it.

Strategies #5: Teach someone else (or yourself)

Do you remember that , in the learning pyramid, 90% of the knowledge acquired was imparted to others?

It can be accomplished by listening to the material you must remember to someone sitting right in front of you Then, you can explain the information you have just have read in your own words.

If you're not able to find someone to assist you in your practice, or if you're embarrassed, you can stand before an mirror and work on your own.

It is, however, recommended to share the experience with someone else, and then inquire about something they were unable to comprehend because it will help you to refresh your memory and respond to their queries.

Strategies #6: Put into practice what you've learned

If you're looking to remember and quickly master new concepts The best method is to practice it or communicate with people who are experts on the subject.

For instance, if you are trying to learn how the instrument, and are looking to memorize chords, you should begin practicing.

If you're interested in learning an entirely new language, you can search for native speakers you can communicate in the language, and then learn more step by step.

You can join discussions forums or threads in which they discuss a certain area you'd like to learn more about, answer questions, share your thoughts, etc.

So your brain will be able to get more deeply into that information and better keep it in mind.

Strategy #7: Be aware of your mood

Your mood plays an significant aspect when it comes to learning and remembering[66. If you're happy is more likely to remember things. This leads to the question how to apply this to reading or studies?

It's as easy to identify a scenario where your mood is the best for reading. Before you begin preparing the environment, shut your eyes and pay attention for a moment. Gradually, you'll recall the atmosphere where you felt relaxed enough to study.

Likely, If your mood is either unhappy or sad it's harder to find the middle point at which concentration is achieved. It's similar to trying to calm a agitated child.

In such a scenario, it's recommended not to push it just let it unfold until you find an optimal state of mind where you can study.

Strategy #8 Stop!

Let your mind let it breathe and let it relax. Take a stroll or lie down on your couch and close the eyes for couple of minutes and then get back to the work of rewriting your lessons.

When you do this you'll have time to go over what you've learned, identify those things you've encountered as difficult and discover methods to improve your memory and recall of different aspects.

Chapter 8: Mastering Exams

The last topic we have to study, and the last requirement you'll have to meet before passing, is the test. Exams are a very stress-inducing time, and it is likely to be one of the most stressful things you've ever experienced to date. It is essential to enter examinations well-prepared, in terms of your knowledge of the subject as well as your mindset. If you enter an exam unprepared and without confidence, you'll be unable to cope with the huge amount of pressure that comes with deadlines and challenging questions. Therefore, you must prepare for two aspects of exams: content of the subject as well as time management.

The few weeks prior to the final exam can be a good time to review the lessons you've learned over the course of the semester and to sharpen your understanding of the material you've learned. It's not a chance to study the entire subject by hand! Many students I've had previously have floated through the whole semester or even the entire term without putting in any effort and then attempted to accomplish this amazing feat. This doesn't work!

If you've been able to keep up-to-date in your assignments, homework and general study through the entire semester this break will provide you with plenty of time to revisit every topic. This should be considered an opportunity to refresh your knowledge, so that you can rewind your thoughts to the subjects that you were first introduced to at the start of the semester. These subjects will require be given the highest amount of attention because you've completed them not too long ago, however each of the topics you've covered must get a couple of hours of revising that consists of reading over your notes and responding to questions about revision to ensure you're confident about them before you take the final test.

Given that you're likely to be taking exams for each the subjects you study, it's going to be difficult to determine who is spent on each. This is a challenging and stressful process. Should you concentrate on the subjects you're most likely to earn a high score for to boost your overall score, or should you concentrate on your least-favorites to ensure you do not fail? It's an balancing action in this regard however the most effective alternative is to have the same level of proficiency in each subject.

The ones that you're sure of already are given (relatively) less attentionto, whereas the ones that are a concern should be given more time to study to. It's more pleasing on your academic transcript to have a consistent number of good scores rather than a sporadic series of very high scores and nearly failing.

Since your tests will undoubtedly be arranged in an arrangement that isn't logical You'll also need to consider that studying for the exams you took earlier will have to be conducted earlier. This is, of course, normal sense, but don't get caught in the trap of just focusing on these tests and, when they're over, it could be that you realize you didn't have enough time to prepare for the remaining tests.

The task of balancing all this research is a difficult task and your feelings are going be stretched beyond their level. It's going to be completely exhausting, and you'll lose the ability to live a normal life. It is crucial to maintain a sense perspectiveand take control of your stress. To stop your overwhelming work load from becoming overwhelming there are a few easy strategies that can be used.

The second one has about your diet. Although a handful of snacks every now and then to keep you energized during your study is fine however, you should avoid placing an entire bag of sweets next to your desk as you'll have to go through them within five minutes. When the sugar rush kicks in, you might be able to take a bit longer to study but you'll become agitated quickly and feel stressed out as it's impossible to concentrate on your studies. This is the same for coffee. Some are fine, but don't count on them to get through the night. If you are overwhelmed by fatigue, rest and get up early in the morning.

Although stress prevention should be your primary goal, it will be normal to experience certain feelings of stress at this period. If you're sitting at your desk working and you start to feel the stress creeping up on you, you should take a moment to breathe and stop. Relax either on your floor, or in your bed, play soothing music, if needed and tell yourself that you'll be prepared and be successful. Repeat this several minutes while you breathe. This is a technique I've found extremely beneficial during times of stress and also refreshing especially when my mind was in need of to take a break.

Exercise is a great way to reduce stress. If you're able to perform just a little bit of exercises in the morning prior to studying, you'll be able to boost brain activity and place you in a good mood. If you're beginning to slip from your current state even some sit-ups or push-ups are enough to help pump the blood flow back into your body and restore your cheerful mood. If I realize that I've been seated on my computer for an extended period of time and I'm beginning to feel grumpy then I'll leap to the floor and perform some push-ups prior to going right on with my work. The results are remarkable and you'll feel the difference and mood instantly.

Time management is the final and most important aspect to managing stress levels. I can't stress the importance of it enough. The most stress can be caused by the feeling of being unprepared for the exam, or your last second attempt at studying before the exam. If you make sure you're fully prepared prior to the exam and you'll be able take the test feeling more relaxed with confidence that you'll be able to get the grades you deserve.

Chapter 9: Action plan to deal procrastination

Perhaps you've experienced the anxiety that results from postponing important tasks. While you might be driven to accomplish something, putting off a task is a habit that can be that is difficult to get rid of.

The good news is that getting over procrastination is much easier than you think. This chapter we provide an action-oriented plan of action to use as a lifesaver any point. Don't put it off for the future. Stop the cycle of procrastination when you've finished this book.

It is normal, when the need to get started on that project is a thought that comes into your head, the task becomes (suddenly) urgent: your filthy clothes that have accumulated or you need to check the email of that crucial customer, the desk appears dirty, you're extremely tired and, of course..

Then you leave and then you started (or continue) with the activity.

We all go through daily life with a multitude of tasks that are unfinished, large and small, crucial or just every day.

Procrastination is like waves that crash against the Pier. Every time, it makes the spring ever fragile (like the intention to start or complete the task you've been putting off).

The only way to solve this problem is to create a powerful wave breaker that will stop the sea of excuses, distractions and inefficiency. Procrastinate is the Latin word "cras" meaning the future or tomorrow.

It is precisely our reasoning when we delay. We postpone things for later and create a vicious circle of guilt and anxiety that causes more stress.

What is the reason we have this habit of delaying?

There are a variety of reasons. The next step is to suggest three of the principal reasons for this:

1-We'd like to get an immediate reward

There are no immediate negative effects (although we'll be paying for it in the future) at the moment, all is well.

For example, lying on the couch can be more relaxing at this point rather than getting out for a workout. It is much easier to check your email to do now than working on your project you've put off for a while. Chocolate cake tastes better today, as is eating vegetables.

2 Overestimate future production

We believe it's fine to delay things since we'll be able to complete it laterand without an reason. We are convinced that the ideal moment is not right now. However, when the time comes we aren't able to finish or worse, without getting started.

3. We fear

This is perhaps the most secret motive. Fear can be a crippling force that keeps us avoid completing a crucial task or task, or performing something that is simple and safe at its own time.

The never-ending loop of procrastination

Do you remember the last time that you delayed something without even realizing? These are the steps you went through:

Excuses

Discomfort

Distraction

First stage: You perceive anxiety or discomfort in front of that activity-what-is-what-to-do.

Second stage: As a rational reaction, your brain attempts to relieve that feeling through an additional task. Thus, you are extremely efficient in other tasks (which aren't a priority at the time).

Third stage: Your brain stores that activity-that-is-what-to-do, as painful and seeks more distractions or some logical reason that explains why you postponed. In that moment all the pleasant excuses come to mind that tomorrow is a different date, and it's important to respond to that email and the appointment was inevitable and, etc. The list goes on and on.

When you come back to think about the task you've put off which you had put off at the beginning, it triggers guilt or remorse , and you are back at the beginning position.

Alongside the guilt and stress that comes with in procrastinating, there are some other repercussions of delaying the task at hand:

• Create a negative image among coworkers, friends and your family.

* Your desire to succeed is no longer there. to achieve.

Failure to meet your goals or get the outcomes you desire.

Risking your health and wellbeing in the case of an exercise that's health-related (such as a check-up every year or a new exercise routine).

The problem is that procrastinating can negatively impact your self-esteem as well as mood. According to a study, the majority of students facing an exam for their finals said they'd like to avoid postponing. The reason for this is that postponing their final exam would cause them to be unhappy.

Whatever the project is, procrastination creates the same feelings. The only way to resolve this issue is to stop the cycle right from the beginning.

Stopping yourself from procrastinating is akin to playing an elementary game

Let's look at an example of an elementary school teacher. As you could imagine, keeping the order of a room with more than 10 children can seem difficult. With his imagination and wit He came up with a plan (which was actually an exercise) to complete the drawing exercise without distraction.

When using coloring pencils with colored inks, the users need to repeat the following phrase"I am coloring I am coloring, It is coloring ....

The game only has 1 rule: When the instructor declares HIGH FREEZE! Everyone must stop coloring and remain silent. In silence and not being frozen! If the teacher hits them, they are able to continue drawing and play the game.

Incredibly, this game is an effective strategy that is also effective for adults:

* Don't delay the crucial task.

* Also, to stay clear of distractions

In the next section, we'll show how to use it in a straightforward manner that you don't have to sing throughout the day.

The most effective method to end procrastination

Let's get started on the game. It's simple to play; there's only one rule you must follow.

If we delay our work it's not that we put off doing something. The real reason is that we are extremely productive at other activities that aren't essential at the moment.

We switch that activity to another one that will keep us busy. This is the reason this strategy is effective. If you're not involved in the activity you are working on, you can't do anything else. It's an illusion. It's also a very effective trick.

Before you start to reply to an unimportant email, go online to watch an online video on YouTube or read an article or avoid the task then stop and put the task on hold and. If your mind is tempted to wander off into the cloud for a second but it's not possible to progress or start this task, it's okay. But do not do anything other than that.

This way you'll be more disciplined. If you fail to perform the task you are required to do, you will have no other choice. When you use this method it will stop you from being productive in other tasks that you are merely trying to complete that waiting to be completed.

It appears like a waste of your time since you're doing nothing. However, in reality it's training your brain. This way you'll be able to control your thoughts. If you are faced with something you need to accomplish, you're just doing it. It's like a powerful break wave that can be used to procrastinate and to distract yourself.

Stop the stalemating waves with this method, and then manage to complete the most important tasks.

If you try this amazing technique, you are unable to stop the waves of procrastination it is likely that you need to work to become better disciplined throughout your daily life.

In reality, discipline is the most important tool for overcoming distractions and effectively finish (without delay) every task you begin.

10 Strategies to Avoid procrastinating

1 Follow your rule that says 10 minutes
The rule of 10 Minutes states that if you're thinking of an action that could be completed within fewer than 10 minutes, you should not make it a priority. Create it happen. It is possible to extend that duration to 15-20 minutes. When you establish this routine into a routine you will have many tasks you won't have the chance to delay.

2-Take a tiny first step: If, for example, you are scared of doing something due to any reason, you might consider doing it for 10 minutes, then take it off. As soon as you start to work you feel less anxious and you find the courage to keep working and complete the task. The first step is the one that you take. you can overcome the resistance and begin seeing things which appeared impossible to you. Don't think about it and just do it.

3-Routines are helpful When you transform monotonous and tedious chores into routines you'll be able to complete things with minimal effort. Routines are routines or habits that you carry out almost invisibly and make life easier.

4 Make choices You often put off the task without thinking about it because you aren't able to think about the issue. Spend a few minutes to consider what the task is really about and decide on a solution. You can decide to put off the task in a rational manner and in that case, you're not delaying the process and will not be embarrassed about it.

5-Track your time: Record in a notebook the tasks you accomplish each day, and the amount of time you've devoted to each. By recording your time you build a personal commitment which makes you more accountable in the way you spend your time.

Learn to say no A lot of the obligations that you delay are commitments that you've wished to fulfill because you aren't sure how to say no.

7. Don't be afraid to quit: It might not be the right time to complete something. Sometimes, we think we must do

something because we've begun it. If time changes the project and it becomes not as relevant or even significant enough, then just stop it and get on with other tasks. Do not delay your work by putting it off.

8- Manage your energy and rather than your schedule: It's essential that you work at your peak. If you're exhausted or are down, the chances of putting off work increase significantly. To be more positive you should rest, manage your food intake and workout.

9-Use Seinfeld's method: Jerry Seinfeld, actor and comedian, employs that strategy to write jokes each day. If you are required to complete something each day, you should use an agenda and mark it with an X each day you complete it. The aim is not just to end the chain that runs through the calendar.

10-Divide the work into smaller and tangible tasks: A huge and complex task can be overwhelming. When you divide it into smaller tasks, you can be able to see the road ahead clearly and the hesitation to tackle it lessens.

Chapter 10: Other Study Techniques

The days where it was sufficient to go to your classes and complete your assignments before taking your tests you had to go through your textbooks, notes, and even your course are over. With the advancement of technology and resources that are now accessible to all students are expected to perform a lot better for themselves. Your instructors will guide students and help you navigate diverse courses and subjects and courses, providing guidance to the right direction and providing suggestions. They should be available to to talk about any aspects of your work in which you have difficulty. They are not able to offer you all the data that is available or be competent to instruct on the best study strategies that are most effective for you. You have to research the details for yourself and take advantage of them to your maximum benefit.

What type of learner Are you?

First, you must determine what kind of person you are. Are you a person who learns by listening, or someone who is an auditory-based learner? If yes, you could find yourself taking notes in your textbooks or reading them with your mouth and talking about them with others can help you remember the details. You could also think about recording your notes or important points and playing them in the future. One benefit is that you are able to listen to them while you're walking to lectures, traveling on public transportation, or at other times you'd typically be wasting time studying.

Do you learn via being an a visual learner? By using different colors and noting important aspects in your notes and textbooks can help you remember the information, and so do drawing diagrams, sketches as well as mind-maps. Simply highlighting important points in a random manner but it will not help you! It is essential to remain focussed and concentrate on the information you are noting.

You could also be in the less common category of an a tactile learner, which is often referred to as a kinesthetic student. This implies that your style of learning is more suited to physical activities rather than listening to lectures or watching videos or demonstrations. So, by physically performing something, playing roles and making models will help you concentrate into consideration the key concepts more effectively.

Make the most of your classes

If possible, study the subject of the lecture that you're scheduled to attend before the class. This can be of advantage, since by doing it, you'll know the subject matter, and it can also help you come up with questions you might want to ask should they not be addressed during the lecture.

If the lecture is also going to review the points of the previous lecture review the notes you took during the class to refresh your memory as well as take note of any concerns you've come up with after attending the lecture.

If you are a student who falls into the category of auditory learners recording lectures in order you can have them heard in the future is a great idea. "PerfectNotes" provides a fantastic recording of lectures and notes tool that allows you to go back and review your recordings and notes at any time you require. It's unlikely that you'll be able to record all the information the lecturer has to say or says, and you shouldn't attempt to do this. If you attempt this, you'll get too busy taking notes that you won't have the time to fully grasp the content being discussed or think about the information or ask questions. It is important to take as precise notes as you are able without distracting yourself from the actual lecture. After the lecture is over review your notes quickly and, if you are able to talk about them with other students in order to gain additional clarity and understanding. In the future, when you have more time available it is possible to to edit your notes if it will aid you, or just make them more current by making notes or underlining key aspects. When writing your notes, ensure they are clear and well-spaced to allow you to add additional information later in the event that you want to in the future, and that you don't have to revise them in the future. If the handout will be handed out following the slide show or will be made available via "BlackBoard," do not take the time to write down precise notes on the information that is going to be given to you in the future.

Learn the most from your Lecturer

Your lecturer is a professional educator who has chosen this profession based on their preferences and because it is one with that they have a strong connection. It is important to make the most use of your lecturer's expertise and expertise as you can. Be noticeable by asking questions, and demonstrating an enthusiasm for the subject and ask for assistance in the event of a difficulty. People like to interact with others with similar values and have similar interests and lecturers are no exception. If you demonstrate an interest in the subject that they teach, and contribute with a sense of humour and ask intelligent questions the lecturers will be impressed by your efforts. They will have more interest in your contribution and the work you do as opposed to an individual in behind in the class who is unable to make a significant contributions during the lectures. Additionally when it comes down to marking papers, a lecturer usually goes through the pile of papers they need to grade without much consideration of the person who wrote the piece. However lecturers will examine papers written by students they've come to know and want to see do well. They're likely to spend more time marking these paper, adding suggestions, and adding marks where they could.

Resolving Boring Work

If you're being asked to study a subject you don't really enjoy or a compulsory subject that is part of your curriculum, it may seem very hard to remain excited, engaged and not get distracted from other areas that are more exciting in your study. The first step is to realize that you have to work through this issue. Make sure to focus on the positive aspect of things and if you are able to succeed in completing this assignment then you are able to proceed to more exciting areas of your study. Imagine all the opportunities which are bound to become available to you should you be able to successfully finish the course. When you're completed with this boring assignment and you'll never be required to do it ever again. The Pomodoro method is a method to tackle boring tasks. It's a technique in that you work in short periods of approximately 25 minutes, in which time you must complete some task you've assigned yourself. It may appear like you're not making progress on the work that has to be completed. Your efficiency, however, must be high and the quantity of work done will eventually grow.

Flash cards

The flash cards are around for many years, they are helpful for testing your memory on important facts and are an excellent revision tool. Flash cards are portable and allow you to carry them around on hand to use when and when you've got some spare time, such as when you're waiting for a bus or waiting for your lecture to start. It's no surprise that you're now additionally able to purchase the software for flash cards. It is usually free and can be used on various mobile phones and personal computers. The software in most cases provides sets of cards that have been designed to cover specific topics, and the option of creating your own set if want to. The pre-packaged cards as well as any sets you make your own can be printed you wish to. Studystack.com is one of the sites that offers this service.

Mnemonics

Make use of mnemonics in order to remember large chunks or lists of data or even rules. Mnemonics can be used to organize information into a format that makes it easier for your brain to remember and recall by the usage of acronyms and memorable terms phrases, or words, as well as other techniques. For example, if you are studying French you need to know when you should use the pronouns tu and you, both of which refer to "you." Utilizing the abbreviation FRAC it is easier to remember to use tu when speaking to someone you know, such as a family member or animal.

Research Papers more effectively

In the first place, if offered a selection of tasks pick the one you find to be most interesting and one that you are comfortable with. If you're interested in the assignment, it won't feel like an overwhelming task and you're more likely to avoid putting off the task. Be sure to know the purpose behind the essay will require your essay. It's very easy to divert your attention from the subjectand write in a way that is not your knowledge and the subject you'd like to write about.

It can be a long-winded process therefore it is crucial to get started at it as soon as you receive the assignment. But before you head out to your library begin exploring the Internet take a moment to think about the information you would like to include in your assignment, and which questions you'll have to find out the answer. When you have these details along with a rough outline of your task, you are able to browse the Internet for a directory of experts in the subject, as well as the most reliable references on the subject to assist you write your essay. Check to see if they're available at the library you are using, and if they're not, then ask your library to request the books from another library, in the event that they have such a service.

In addition to reference books as well as reference books, in addition to reference books, Internet is a great sources of data. However internet access Internet is also extremely demanding, since there's generally plenty of rubbish to be discovered among the best sources.

Companies like Microsoft or Google have for a while recently been investing huge amounts of money in order to ensure that their engines are the top selection. This has significantly increased the number of results that are returned to us for our queries by moving those less relevant pages towards the bottom of the results that are returned. You can cut down your Internet time spent researching by identifying all the terms you're likely to want to hunt for and then making use of Boolean search to obtain better results in your searches. Another way to save time is to utilize "Pocket" which can save webpages, articles or videos you think could contain valuable information. "Pocket" is an easy to use program that allows you to store all web information in one place at the pressing of one button. The most effective method to organize your research materials is to browse through any pages you think might be useful and, if they appear interesting, save the pages into "Pocket" and then go onto the next item within the results generated by your search. Once you've exhausted your research do you look over thoroughly the content you saved. This way you won't be shifting from the Internet to note-taking as well as with "Pocket," the content you've saved is accessible whenever you decide to remove it.

Read carefully, then reread and finally take a look at the summary

A great way to remember important information found in textbooks or reference books is to first go through the content to gain an overview and an comprehension of the material. After you've done that take a look at what you've read and what areas you consider to be the most significant, or will require more focus. Read the text again and read it slower this time taking notes of important terms and concepts. After you've completed the second reading and feel confident that you've grasped the subject, write a summary of the material in your own terms. It is essential to compose these summaries using your own words, not simply copying portions of the text. When you write your summary in yourself, you'll have a greater chance to retain the details than if you were copying a few sections from the book. They will also be beneficial to refer to later when you write assignments as well as to help you revise your work.

Effective essay writing

After you've identified the topic for your paper, contemplated the details you wish to include in your assignment, and done your research, you have to determine what you want to include in your essay. First, write everything you have thought of and thoughts on paper, and then arrange them into a clear order. It is possible to do this by creating a list, and noting the items according to their importance as well as the category of your essay that they fall within. You can also make this happen using an outline or flow chart, depending on what is most suitable for your needs.

The introduction establishes the tone of an essay, so make sure to create an engaging introduction. If not, the reader won't be attracted or their attention piqued. The introduction should clearly state the main purpose of the essay and not exceed the length of the essay. If it's too long, the reader could be bored waiting to the details of the essay. However, it should provide enough information to allow readers to have an idea of the main purpose that the article is attempting to achieve.

Your essay's body should be designed to elaborate on your introduction, and fulfill all expectations that readers have learned from the introduction and the table of content If you have one. The body is where the structure is most important and where your previous work on the structure of your essay will be rewarded. It is important to ensure that your content is relevant engaging, informative, and carefully thought-out and includes solid explanations, examples, and references.

The conclusion serves to recap briefly the content you wrote within the main body your essay and also to emphasize the most significant points and arguments. The conclusion is not the right place to make new arguments or arguments If you find yourself doing this, you have to locate the proper location within the body of your essay in which to place these ideas. Check your conclusion against your introduction, because they must be very identical in their content. introduction should outline what you're planning to write about, and your conclusion summarizing the content you've written.

Once you've finished the essay you wrote, you will need to proofread and edit it in the way you think is appropriate. If you can, complete this review the next day you've finished writing the essay to ensure that you are viewing the essay with a fresh set of eyes. Use the spell-checker on your word processor. Also, make sure you are using the correct grammar, substitute words you often use with a good synonym, and refrain from using complicated words or jargon. If you don't comply, you'll appear unprofessional and create the impression of lack of attention to detail that will not impress to your instructor.

If you don't have a compelling reason to not make sure you type your assignments and essays. Select a font which can be read easily for example, Arial or Times New Roman, rather than choosing a more artistic font that is difficult to read. Your instructor wants to be able to read the work and make notes swiftly and efficiently, not determining your personality based on the characteristics of the font that you've selected.

Share what you've learned with your family and friends.

An effective method of reaffirming the knowledge you've acquired and ensuring you have a thorough understanding of the subject is to discuss the subject you're learning with your friends or relatives. If you're not able to help them comprehend the concepts or respond to their questions with ease, you'll know that you must learn more about the subject and you will have a better idea of the areas in which your knowledge was lacking.

Make sure to apply the lessons you've learned to your daily day

This isn't feasible for every subject However, when it is possible, make sure to put the knowledge you've learned to use in your daily routine. This will aid in memory retention, aid in increase your knowledge and experience and make the subject you're studying much more engaging. For instance, if are taking a course in Economics and you have just finished studying forex and its function that it plays within the world economy Take note of the importance by keeping track of the price of gold and the rate of exchange for your currency in relation to other currencies. Instead of just observing that the rate or price has changed by analyzing what you've learned and some additional study, try to discover your own reasons for the changes. You might find the subject fascinating enough that you think of trading FOREX or other commodities as a hobby or perhaps exploring it as a potential career.

Past Papers

It is recommended to take copies of your past papers from the past three years, for a variety of reasons, with the most obvious being to test your understanding. Alongside responding to them, you must take note of the subjects and questions that seem to be asked frequently. Examining boards typically employ the same examiner for each subject year on year and the examiner is likely to have specific sections of the syllabus which they consider to be the most crucial and prefer to pay attention to when writing the examination questions. With this knowledge it is possible to give the most importance to these areas in your planning of revision. Be sure to go through the entire syllabus. Examiners shift frequently and have their own way of preparing exams and their own opinions regarding the most significant content. If you limit your revision to topics included in the exam questions over the past three years, you're taking a risk and could possibly be found out.

Chapter 11: the Magic Of Speed Reading

When someone has to study and keep track of a large amount of knowledge in very short timeframe, they want they could experience something that was magical. If you're also among them do not fret because there's something that is magical and can allow you to grasp a large amount of information in a short time. It's called Speed Reading.

What exactly is Speed Reading?

It's a way to be able to identify and comprehend the phrases and sentences that are on a page in a short time instead of navigating through each word.

The average person read about 250 words per minute (wpm) however, this rate can increase, double, or quadruple in speed reading.

The benefits of speed Reading

Speed reading has many wonderful advantages. A few of them include:

*Speed reading will save your time without having to sacrifice information.

If you read faster the speed of your brain is improved. It helps you retain more information over a longer period of time.

*Speed reading results in an unshakeable mind. This means the information you read is processed swiftly and effectively.

*Speed reading improves concentration. When the brain process an enormous volume of content in a shorter time, the risk of being distracted are minimal.

*Since your brain's muscle, exercise aid in strengthening it. Speed reading is an example of such exercise.

Strategies that will Master Speed Reading

Learning the technique of fast reading achievable for everyone even for you. There are three ways to master speed reading. Choose the one that fits your needs most. Let's look at them:

1. Pointer Method

When you use this method, you make use of your finger index to move through the words you're reading. Evelyn Wood was one of the very first people to pioneer speed reading. in the 50s Evelyn was able to write up to 2,700 words per minute using this method.

The other terms used to describe this technique are "meta guidance" or "hand Pacing" method. It aids in reading speed since your brain also works in a coherent manner when your finger moves. Since your eyes follow the finger you stay clear of distractions.

This also stops readers from skipping back (going back and reading sentences or words) the text, and also helps readers save significant amounts of time reading.

2. Scanning Method

This method lets you swiftly move your eyes over the text, and you can quickly identify key sentences or phrases. It is possible to keep the motion that your eye is moving from right to left however, the most efficient way is in the middle.

This technique alters the traditional method of reading from the left to right in an article. The focus shifts on the top and the bottom.

This technique helps you focus your attention on key words like numbers, names or other important words. In this way you can save a considerable period of time.

3. Perceptual Expansion Method

The goal of this method is to enhance you're peripheral sight. The typical reader will concentrate on a single word at a time when studying, however this technique helps your brain be able to read more words at once.

It is evident that the fixation time is similar during perceptual growth, however the amount of words you fixate your eyes on increases. Your brain gets more information at the same time.

When compared with the other two methods It is more hard to grasp.

However, mastering this method will yield the most effective outcomes.

Note Speed reading techniques share one thing in common. They block any "self-vocalization" of the words. This means that you can avoid the vocalization and listening to each word that comes into your head when reading a book.

When should I speed read?

It's a problem that is often asked by those who want towards speedreading. There are many ways to speed read, however many people aren't sure what speed reading is or whether they should be speed reading at all.

To be able to achieve efficient and effective time-reading, there needs to be a good equilibrium between speed as well as understanding. A few studies have revealed that speed reading does not provide an efficient method when you need to keep track of specifics for a long period of duration.

Avoid the speed-reading when you are confronted with the following issues:

*Texts that are complex like legal or technical documents

* If you are reading an unfamiliar or novel text

* If you need to learn something new and impart the similar thing to someone else

* If you must remember the details

The question is unanswered. It is best to accelerate your reading when you need to comprehend only the conclusion or the fundamental arguments that are given in a piece of information.

This also implies that speed reading is advantageous in situations where you must read the same thing slowly while you're not in a rush. The second reading will improve the comprehension of your reading since you are already aware of what you're reading.

Strategies to Increase the Speed of Reading

If you'd like to use speed reading the first step to mastering how to learn, here are some suggestions to increase your speed reading skills.

* Stay away from distractions

It is recommended to speed read in a space that is free of interruptions and distractions. It helps you concentrate exclusively on the words and phrases you are reading.

* Rehearse

Practice before beginning with speed reading. To do this, pick up an entire novel and read using all three techniques that were mentioned earlier. Determine which one works best for you, and which method you can understand and remember the best. If you have found the most effective one, you can speed read using it.

* Pay attention to the relevant Words

While you read at a fast pace take note of when you see relevant phrases or words. Reduce your speed at these points and try to get the maximum information, and then continue to move swiftly.

* Avoid Repetitive Reading

When you are speed reading, make sure to make sure you cover the majority of terms you've previously read. This will stop your eyes from returning to earlier words you read. In addition, your speed of reading will not decrease.

* Practice

If you are looking improve your speed-reading skills, do some practice till it is your preferred method of reading.

Chapter 12: Chunking Technique

Students are always interested in how they can build a strong memory. In the end, it's crucial to learn to be able to remember, absorb, and recall the information they learn in their classes.

There is a method to boost memory that can help improve memory by the artful use of data grouping. This is known as Chunking Technique. Chunking Technique.

This chapter explains what Chunking Technique is used. Chunking Technique is used and what benefits can be derived from it.

Chunking Technique Defined. Chunking Technique Defined

Chunking is the process of cutting up large chunks of information and arranging them into simple-to-remember pieces. This is a method that is frequently employed by students to aid students remember complex concepts and difficult-to-understand words.

The reason for this was the inherent weaknesses of our short-term memory. We can typically be able to process and recall 4-7 things in the short term memory. The brain is bombarded with massive chunks of information in one go is like doing an overload for your brain's short-term memory.

Your brain must process the information into smaller bits to allow it to process it and then remember them quickly. This is why chunking can be an effective method to improve memory. The brain doesn't get shocked when they discover a plethora of information being absorbed at once.

A few examples of this technique are:

* Splitting numbers into smaller groups. For instance, phone numbers can be separated instead of keeping the entire list in one place. (555)5554321 can be translated as (555) 5555 4321.

* Assigning letters or numbers to numbers, much as how acronyms and mnemonics operate. The four learning styles that are commonly used are simpler

to remember with the use of an acronym like VARK is employed: Auditory, Visual Reading/Writing and Kinesthetic.

Linking difficult-to-remember information with other objects. For example, you could recall the salt-water interactions in the human body through visualizing Mary Had A Little Lamb nursery rhyme. "Wherever salt goes, the water moves" could be translated to Mary (salt) accompanying Lamb (water) wherever she travels.

The Chunking Technique is getting better

Here are some helpful tips to implement the technique of chunking efficiently into your study tools:

Begin slowly. Break information down into small pieces, and then as you're comfortable, you can try expanding these chunks so that you retain more.

Seek out important connections between items you have in your groupings of information. Understanding how words or numbers are related to one another will help you recall them easily.

Try mixing chunking and other strategies for memory to enhance your recall and retention. You can use keywords in an mnemonic, and then connect the idea with simple-to-remember things.

You might be studying about the foods you should eat to help with the control of blood pressure. You can make an mnemonic GLOBSY POD, which means:

Garlic

Leafy greens

Oatmeal

Beets

Fish that are omega-3 and Salmon

Yogurt

Pistachios

Olive oil

Dark chocolate

Then, you imagine the large tube that is full of blood, which the levels slowly decrease when you recite the GLOBSY Food mnemonic.

The use of mnemonics and visualizations can help you to retain concepts and procedures. Combining these techniques can assist in improving your long-term memory.

Chapter Wrap-Up

Chunking is a fantastic way to take in large amounts of details. It involves breaking up information into smaller pieces by using links, data groupings acronyms, mnemonics and even visualizations. This technique takes away loads on the brain, allowing to process information effectively and speedily. Retention and recall can also be improved by using the chunking technique.

Chapter 13: How do Online Classes Work

The first step is by understanding what online classes are. Online learning is a method of sharing information via the internet, and helping students develop new skills through the internet. Learn online each time you do a Google or YouTube searches that are related to a subject, however classes online are more focused and concentrated as instead of having separate subjects, you must master the entire course from start to finish, make notes and write tests.

Make sure you are digitally organized

The primary distinction between an online classroom and a traditional classroom is that you're responsible in the educational environment. You are responsible for setting the study space and the device you use to study, such as a smartphone or computer as well as any other equipment or software you might require.

In the majority of cases the majority of cases, any smartphone or computer with internet access is sufficient. However, some classes may require more sophisticated hardware, such as video editing, animation, or modeling. You'll need a computer with a adequate configuration to run these kinds of software. Don't register for any online courses until you have a good understanding of the technical prerequisites. If you're not able to be sure of meeting them, put off the course until you have the time to plan them or go with free online resources.

Certain online classes might require headphones to enjoy presentations without distractions or a printer so that you can make copies of the documents shared. In any case, be sure that you've got the right technical specifications before starting the class.

Plan ahead for your classes and establish a routine of checking in early. I would suggest that you familiarize yourself with the software for virtual classrooms and study the various tools offered to you, including private chatting, notes from the community or the ability to record your class. Make sure you know which mute buttons can be found, as this could help you avoid embarrassing situations.

Use Tricks to Activate Your Brain (Treat online classes as live lectures)

This year , as a lot of colleges and schools are shifting towards online-only learning and you'll be taking lots of classes via video conferencing software such as Zoom, Google meet, or Hangouts. That means that you'll be doing an extensive amount of asynchronous education because you'll be assigned lots of work assignments for reading, assignments to complete, and you'll have to complete these at home. If you're taking an individual online class , everything is autonomous and the issue with this remote, asynchronous and independent nature of online classes is that you are likely to get in the lagging category if you're not self-controlled. Classes in person are conducted in the person and run in a specific time frame and this helps you to keep track of your homework and reading assignments. In addition it helps to organize your schedule however, with online classes, much of the structure is missing.

Treat online classes as if they were real classes in terms the schedule and the place you are taking them. Make your brain believe the online courses are legitimate, and should not be skipped. To do this we will look at the factors that affect your class in person such as fixed classrooms, uniforms, fixed rooms or your preferred class dress code, or the learning setting. To duplicate this, you must fix an area first in which you'd like to go to online classes. We tend to be able to do a variety of things in the same location. We eat meals in our bedrooms, sit in our living rooms, watch TV and study on our sofa or bed. Every location should be linked to a specific task that will provide you with the motivation to focus on this particular task.

Therefore, it is crucial to determine the exact location you'll be doing your online research so that when you reach the specific location within your home, your brain is tricked to believe that it is the classroom or the place for learning. If you are doing multiple things in the same location it could be causing you to feel sleepy in your bedroom or cause you to feel hungry if it's in which you eat or where your thoughts be diverted if it's your relaxation space. Many people don't have a huge home or a separate study space However, the intention isn't to go into a separate room, instead of a separate area, therefore a small table and chair by the bed can be sufficient however, make sure the your space is not being used for other activities such as eating or watching films.

Then there's the uniform or your preferred classroom attire. Whenever you are taking online classes, you should be sure you wear the identical uniform or dress you would wear to classes in person This will allow your brain into the zone of learning.

Uniforms play an important part in the classroom; this is the reason why so many businesses have strict guidelines for the type of attire that should wear at work. When you shop, you have the opportunity to look at different sections both formal and informal so when you're wearing the correct attire, you won't feel the need to be performing any other task other than studying. Think about the number of times you've been to a movie in your uniform , and you'll be able to understand.

The next step is the learning environment or study areas Let us look at the study spaces to your classes in person There must be an office chair or chair cum table, and your notebook along with your stationery and water bottle. In your learning space you must keep the same things that you have in your classroom, nothing more and nothing more. clearing your study space creates more space for you to focus and helps you focus. We'll discuss creating smart study spaces later on in this publication, yet the premise will remain the same: maintain order and keep it clear.

Learn to organize your information digitally

When you attend in-person classes, you'll write down your lessons in a notebook. Most likely keep a separate notebook for each subject however, as more information is digital, it's crucial to learn how to work from online files and also take notes online. If you're the type of person who saves everything to their desktop and creates a massive collection of data, it is necessary to create a separate folder on your hard drive to accommodate each course you're attending and then create a subfolder of every task you're working on in the class that has multiple files with it. In addition, in your online note-taking program, you need to keep a notebook online for each class . Whether you're writing notes with pencil on paper and scanning them, or using a tablet or typing them into your computer, you must have a designated place where all your notes or every class gets organised and saved on your smartphone or computer.

Create a Study Space

There are two primary aspects to consider when designing your workspace, the separation of space and isolating. Separation is the concept of creating a space with one function, space that's exclusively used for research as well as having a second space to relax or engage in other activities. The environment has some influence on our mental state. Therefore, it is important to ensure you don't need to fight against your surroundings to remain focused. In the words of Jay Shetty tells in his book Think Like a Monk, "Location is energy-rich and Time is memory." Every location is linked to the energy needed to complete something specific when you are doing the same thing during the same period, and in the same location every day, it will be a memory in your subconscious mind and it becomes a breeze to perform that task every day for instance, in the event that you rise at a reasonable hour in the morning, and begin learning in a particular area to learning each day It will be effortless for you to complete every day without distractions.

The second thing to do is to stay away from any people who may interrupt your study, and , honestly, this can be an issue when you live with your family. If you're fortunate that you have dedicated space for studying then you can shut the doors to that space and remain in the space. However, what happens do you do if there isn't enough space to create a private space for studying? If space is scarce or you're not sure what to do, think up a creative idea and build an interim partition in your space or find an area in your home that is quiet and, in general, do not confront anything that can be expected to distract you such as windows, TVs, etc. If you are forced to stand in front of the wall with a blank space, you can do so. In any case you have the option to play around and determine what works for you.

In order to handle interruptions from your family or other people living within the same area as you live, you must be in good contact with family members to let them know about your studies. However, there are other adjustments you can create in your study space which can be helpful also. One of them is why you should put up the DND sign. You could put up a similar type of system to inform your family members know that you're trying to concentrate and that they shouldn't interrupt your study.

If you're unable to find a sense of isolation, you may look for another option is available at any to use at any time. If you aren't able to set up an permanent space it is possible to begin by creating a temporary space every day with a tiny table and a chair. You could even incorporate this into the routine of your routine. Pick the best time of day to study online, that is most suitable for you. Maybe you're more productive in the mornings or you prefer to study in the evening, and you're more comfortable studying in the evening. Figure the best time for you and adhere to it. In both the that you're distracted in the early morning and at night are minimal, and you'll have the privacy you seek.

Additionally, these are qualities that a good study space should possess:

"Light": A dim room may feel crowded and depressing. This can cause fatigue and strain on your eyes when you stare at your screen for an extended period of duration. If you don't have the right lighting arrangement in your home, you might want to consider making use of portable sources of light.

"Ergonomics": If you are sitting on the ground with your laptop upon your knees you're likely end up suffering from discomfort in your back and back of your body. The ergonomic study space allows you to focus on material you're studying. If you're uncomfortable the pain and stiffness can hinder your study and reduce your ability to concentrate.

* Materials Prior to settling down to an online class make sure you have everything you'll need to be at ease throughout your time. I suggest keeping your water bottle as well as a coffee flask if are a coffee enthusiast as well as some fruits such as banana or apples to satisfy your cravings. Be sure to avoid eating anything spicy or something that could cause discomfort or insomnia in your study.

Find your Learning Objectives and Objectives

Your objective must be precise and clearly defined. Only will you be able to keep your own discipline For instance when your aim is to master coding however, this is rather general and not very specific. instead , define your goals such as"by the end of the day I will be able to perform simple addition operations with java or python or whatever language you plan to study. Setting a goal for every day can help you get better each day and will keep you motivated to learn, since, without a sense of achievement it is possible to lose interest in the goal. The goal could simply be completing the lesson and being able to complete all the issues at the close of the chapter, or exam questions from the previous year. When you decide to set a target, ensure that you establish a timeframe to attain those goals without a deadline your mind will tend to delay the task.

If a teacher or professional is creating an online course, they may have multiple objectives for students. It is crucial to set your objectives and schedule with your teacher however, simultaneously, make sure to read the material thoroughly at the end of each class to ensure that you are able to comprehend the subject thoroughly and be able to meet your objectives. Once you've identified your objectives and goals, it is crucial to note them down, most likely in a location close to the area where you work or an outline on your desk. Check them daily before you start studying class material or study your notes to track your performance. Keep track of the important milestones you accomplish over the course of the semester Be sure to reward yourself after you have reached every mark. The reward could be as simple as an ice cream treat or playing your favourite game.

The Study should be able to set time limits. Study

A way to boost productivity is to force yourself to work for a certain amount of time, and to be able to focus only for a short period of time. You could set a timer that will last 30 minutes to study When the timer expires take a break to walk around then return at your workstation for an additional 30 mins. If you repeat this procedure two times, you'll be able to say you've spent an hour studying for all of it. In technical terms is known by"the Pomodoro Technique.

The online study can trigger eyes fatigue, so taking breaks will provide some rest to your eyes. You can also do some stretching to remove your mind of any stiffness or mental block before returning to reading.

However, ensure that you do your research for the entire amount of time you believe is required to accomplish your objectives and cross every task off your list.

Learn to manage distractions

When learning online it is crucial to avoid distractions from digital sources because the majority of internet content is created to draw people's attention. When you are studying online, make sure that you are using the internet for only specific reasons, and that is written out clearly before you on an adhesive note. When you're distracted, look at the note and remind you not to divert your attention from the reason you are using the internet for. Sort things into important and urgent. You can employ an approach called the Eisenhower Method, popularized by Stephen Covey's book First Things First, to identify the distinction between important and urgent tasks. Notifications can be urgent, however they're never really important. An Harvard Business Review article about the expense of constantly checking notifications says that numerous University studies have revealed that refocusing your attention after being distracted by emails could take as long as 20 minutes. Therefore, you should switch off notifications on your phone or computer in order to not waste time. If you are not self-controllable and are unable to control your behavior, you can utilize various tools to disable notifications for a specific period of time and track the time spent on a specific action to look back at it later and make self-corrective steps.

Even when you are distracted, set a schedule to avoid distractions. If you're caught up in any communication such as a friend or relative, set the timer to distract yourself or keep the glass sandglass. When your time to distract is up, you can return to your studies immediately. However, getting distracted too many times could distract you from the goal, so you should make sure you reduce the amount of times you are distracted in the time that . No matter what happens it is important to adhere to the timer you've set for your studies.

Create an Calendar to study Calendar

Learning online must be organized. Make a calendar that can aid you in remembering all important dates such as deadlines for exams or deadlines to submit your assignments. It's possible to keep your calendar on your desktop , or on your smartphone, or by hand on the form of a paper-based sheet. If you're attending classes that are in a different zone, be sure to add that to your calendar. Start by incorporating the times and duration of the classes online into your schedule. Then, design your own study time to coincide with your classes. This will include the time needed to prepare for a class, and also time blocks for reviewing the lesson once it has occurred. After that, you should create a weekly session during which you will review the study guides, or summaries of the lecture content so far.

You should also set an amount in your calendar to determine when you must start studying and when you must leave the study mode, and then set an alarm on your phone that will be alerted for the specific hours. After you've set these basic time blocks on your calendar, you can choose to designate a particular time for exercising or read, catch up on your favourite shows or just hang out with your loved ones.

Be on Time

The consequences of procrastination are fatal to studying online, therefore ensure that you're organized and that you're not slowing down in your online course. If you're having difficulty getting your assignments completed in time, get in touch with your instructor and inform them to help to keep your schedule consistent and clear the backlog. Additionally, you should note notes during online classes rather than taking notes after the class to ensure that you do not have to spend time taking notes after class.

Make To-Do lists

The to-do list could be your guide during your online course of study. It can assist you to keep the track of your progression. Also, you can enjoy the satisfaction of crossing each item off after you have completed it.

According to your preference You can create broad or very short lists. If you prefer, details create a step-by-step to-do list or you can combine various items to make a short list. It is also possible to use whiteboards in which you can record important items to complete for the day as well as the times that you are taking online courses to remind you of your schedule.

Chapter 14: Time Management Tips

Alongside the psychology section This is among the most crucial sections of this book. Time management is usually an essential aspect of any extremely efficient student. When I refer to "time management" I'm not referring to putting the study ahead of anything else. I don't want you do this! I would like you to not be forced to sit for long hours studying, and you can have a life! Below are some helpful tips to help you achieve that.

Hack #1

Make use of the snowball technique when you're overwhelmed with assignments to do.

It's actually something I snatched from the world of personal finance way back in the day and it's completely not related to learning. It's nevertheless a effective remedy for that feeling of total despair when you're faced with an overwhelming amount of work to do that you do not know how be able to finish it by the deadline.

IN A NUTSHELL: When you have tons of homework, organize it from smallest/fastest/easiest to hardest/longest. Begin with the smaller ones then work your way up.

Why? The snowball technique is actually an effective psychological trick. If you have five assignments due to 5 different subjects, it's easy to be overwhelmed with fear , because it appears impossible that anything can ever be completed. You glance at your pile of work and find endless hours of labor ahead. Then you close your computer. It's put off. Then you're crying and screaming at the last minute and then turning in Cand work.

The primary benefit of the snowball technique is that it assists you begin. Beginning with the smaller tasks first helps you get going in the beginning, and when there are many things to accomplish beginning is crucial.

The most crucial thing in the snowball method is the momentum. We've all experienced this before: that sensation of being in a state of the edge of a volcano and invincible - that feeling of slamming your assignments and nothing will stop you from doing it. That's momentum.

The snowball technique helps to create the momentum you need to create. If you complete some smaller tasks and then reach the bigger things, you're on the right track, at full speed.

How? Determine what's the most scary to you and place the task at the bottom of the list. Are the assignments that are the most difficult most terrifying? Do you simply dislike long work? Whatever is making you desire to work on it, make it at the end of the list. Most of the time, it will be the same.

Next, work in reverse. Determine the next thing that is most irritating is, and place that in the second row.

Once you've got everything put in order, the most important task is to begin with the assignment that you've decided to do the most easy. Simply start. Even when it's slow. Begin by taking breaks until you've completed. If you don't finish the first obstacle then you'll be unable to build up this momentum later.

Shortcut: This might seem like a shortcut however, trust me when I say that it's. If you're going to get yourself into the snowball game, bring an assignment that isn't due until. The idea is that you'll be at ease that you'll simply be knocking things out of the air all over the place. Why not put in more work while in this position? It's a way to avoid having to return to the rhythm in the future. If you are doing this regularly you may be able to do everything for a couple of hours each week.

Bonus! If you discover that you enjoy the snowball method, you can try its cousin method, which is the technique of avalanches. It is similar to the snowball method , but it is opposite. Instead of beginning by doing the easiest thing first, you begin with one of the toughest.

The concept is that when you've completed the most difficult task you're expected to accomplish everything else the work seems simple. Both methods work, and typically it's just a matter to figuring out which one is the most suitable for your particular studying style. Personally, I like the avalanche approach, but majority of people prefer using the snowball technique. Try them out!

Hack #2

Improve time management by linking study with other activities

Have you ever read the old saying that states that to make something a routine, you must be doing for a whole month? It's the same. Before you put your Kindle down with a sigh of displeasure Let me clarify I'm not saying that you must do it every day!

In all honesty Who would ever wish to do this? I don't think so, and I'd never suggest it. You can incorporate studying into your schedule without having to completely exhaust yourself. It is possible to do this by linking it to other tasks.

IN A NUTSHELL: Choose one thing you do every day (nearly everyday) and do some study at the time you study to establish an positive relationship and a habit.

Why? The process of creating a regular study routine is among the most difficult tasks to complete. Certain people have no difficult time doing it. For instance, my college roommate for instance was up at 7:15 every single day, including Saturdays! work for homework the following day.

It's difficult because you need to keep doing something regularly to establish a routine and everybody hates doing it. It's usually easy to sit through long hours of studying prior to the test than to integrate the study routine into your day.

This advice is about how to incorporate learning into your daily routine in an easy, relaxed method. The way to do this is through the power of association.

Associative phenomena are psychological that "refers to the connection between mental or conceptual states that arise from the similarity between these state."

In the same way, you would like to connect studying with something else.

If you do this whenever you do this thing, however it happens it is, you'll remember to study. This will not only assist you in remembering to do your homework however, it will also establish a positive relationship with learning.

How? Choose something that you do every day (or at least almost every day). The ideal is to choose something you truly enjoy and also something you can do during your studies. For me it was Netflix. I usually spend an hour or so every morning watching the shows I have on Netflix.

Make it a habit for the next month to take the study materials while you are doing that. You don't need to be studying extremely hard or anything else; simply study during this thing. In time, it will be a stress-free but constant routine!

Pro tip! If you want to build a strong bond study with food. Better yet, make it a combination of food and other things. For instance If you consume some chocolate each day and you stream Netflix each day, you can add study time into the equation.

This is especially effective since the brain makes stronger connections with smells and tastes more than other elements.

Chapter 15: Memory aids that will help boost and enhance your memory

"The main lesson in my life that I learned from Diamond's class was that I mold my brain each day, and you too."

Wendy Suzuki Ph.D. World famous neuroscientists

One of the most fascinating discoveries that have been made regarding the brain has been the idea of plasticity. The term "plasticity" basically means that the brain is able to change, both functionally and chemically in response to experiences. in her work Healthy Brain, Happy Life the renowned Dr. Suzuki describes an experiment where they test the concept of plasticity. They chose that they would test the taxi drivers of England who were preparing to get their licence. Each driver was required to learn many street names. They found that the hippocampi of drivers who did well was bigger than those who did not pass. The good news is that we have the capacity to enhance, stimulate, and enhance our brain. The stimulation of the brain by new experiences and information creates new connections, and strengthens existing ones. In contrast in the event that you deprive your brain of stimulating stimuli it actually shrinks. The concept of plasticity is fascinating because it challenges the notion that was held by many for a long time that once you reach the age of a certain point, your brain has become fixed. Everybody is constantly seeking to increase our knowledge and enhance our brains by stimulating it properly.

As a new teacher, I can remember returning home at the end of the day and thinking "I don't know what I'm planning to do next". Luckily, an experienced teacher introduced me to a variety of methods of teaching. It was initially difficult to comprehend because there were more than 75 methods to pick from. The teacher who was seasoned helped me out and advised that the best way to approach it was to learn a tiny amount of strategies instead of being an inexperienced user of hundreds of strategies. In the two years that I was a teacher, I learned around five strategies I used repeatedly time. Strategies made learning enjoyable and enjoyable for my students as well as helped me grow as a teacher. Through the years, I've extended my methods and introduced new strategies. However, by limiting the number of strategies I employed initially I was able master a handful of strategies instead of becoming average in all strategies. This made me an extremely efficient instructor.

Similar to that we will concentrate on a few of techniques for memory. I will guide you through the techniques I have found most beneficial in learning new concepts over the past twenty-five years teaching. You'll benefit from learning only a few methods of memory as opposed to being aware of the many methods.

7 Techniques for Memory (Try for mastering 2, or 3,)

Technique #1: Journey Method

This technique of memory is a great way to learn sequences of events or lists that happen in a series. With practice you can apply this technique to almost everything you have to learn.

Here's how it works.

You choose a route you will travel on in your lifetime. It could be as simple as a journey to the kitchen every morning. In the beginning, you might require writing the route in your notebook. While you are traveling the route in your head, make a list of points of interest or stops along the route. To recall an inventory of items such as people, events, tests or steps to solving math problems it is possible to connect these items, or images of these items along with the stops along your route.

Let's look at an actual world scenario.

What I did with to use the Journey Method (also called the Loci method) to remember the President's names:

In the year that Barack Obama was sworn in as president and inaugurated as president, he was the 44th president of United States. I've tried several times to remember the names and orders of all presidents in the United States. I would print out the list of all the presidents and then begin to read to the top, and then eventually was overwhelmed by the names, and decided to stop. After learning about the journey method of learning, I decided to give it a go to see if it was possible to master all the names with this method. Here's a brief overview of the experiment I conducted and the results.

The first order of business was to print the list of all the presidents. The task was easy, and finished in just two minutes. The next step was to think of an itinerary or a route. I usually run every day, so I chose my favorite route for running. I sketched out the route and attempted to think of 44 landmarks or places. It was soon apparent that 44 landmarks are too many places and my route was way too long. I've always had success using chunking, which is the process of breaking down a huge list or group into smaller, manageable groups. For instance, you could break up a list of fifty items in 10 groups of five or five groupings of 10. I decided to split the presidents' list in groups of 10 to then create four distinct routes. This made the task much easier and made the routes easier to remember. I then sketched each route and wrote down the president's names on the landmarks on the route.

The next step was a bit difficult. The information I have on the lives and times of the first presidents is quite limited. Therefore I had to come up with a unique way to associate Presidents with landmarks. At first I was unsure how to tie the president's name with that landmark. But after thinking for five to ten mins I began to come up with imaginative ideas. For example, I thought of the son of mine Adam on the other location for James

Adams, the second president. The third landmark, that of Thomas Jefferson, I imagined 100 dollar bills. I repeated this process for the first 10 presidents. It took me about 15 minutes but I had pretty was able to have all ten of the presidents in my head after running through my course several time in my mind. I was enthused.

I did this for the following four presidents in a set of ten. The fifteen presidents in the last set were the most easy to connect with landmarks, as I had a basic understanding of their presidency. Each set of 10 took about 20-25 minutes to connect with landmarks and approximately an hour overall.

I was surprised at how quickly I remembered the names while I walked through my trip. It was a bit of a challenge to come up with good associations however it wasn't difficult.

At the point of getting the third and final set of 10 I was more adept at forming these associations, and it started to be fun. As with everything you learn I'll need to go over my route and the presidents many times in order to transfer all 44 presidents ' names into my long-term memory.

Benefits

Improved memorization with this method of memory helped me to recall the 10 list after having gone through the entire procedure just a couple of times.

* Increased recall of lists significantly.

It's much more fun than gazing at a list, and reciting the names.

A disadvantage

A fair amount of preparation time drawing the route , and developing connections.

It can be difficult to establish an association with the location of a landmark.

* Must be memorized to work.

2. Create a mental map by using images

Mind maps are a simple tool that lets you see and sketch what you are learning.

To make a mind map

The first step is drawing a circle around the room and then write your subject inside it.

Then Draw a spoke out of the circle, which explains the principal issue.

* Next, draw branches using this spoke. Additionally, at this point you are able to draw images to help support your idea. It is helpful if the images are humorous, funny or bizarre.

Repeat the process for more branches, and then make each branch different colors.

These two videos show how to make the mind map

Mind Map Tutorial

https://www.youtube.com/watch?v=tAUsZ9eiorY

Mind maps: How to utilize them to help you study?

https://www.youtube.com/watch?v=PxwYcW3E5Mw

Technique #3: Create a sentence or a story

This method is a mix of the method of journey along with mind map. It is extremely effective for retaining a quick outline or diagram. Let me give you an example. Imagine that you must memorize four organelles in the cell that are the cell membrane, mitochondria, ribosome and the lysosome.

1. Define what is the role or function of each organelle.

Step 2: Write an account of how every organelle is performing their task.

I'm writing this at Starbucks and I'm going to make a short story about a cell receiving coffee.

A cell walks through Starbucks. He is a slur, but walks on his outer covering the cell membrane safeguarding him.

He says "I need some sugar because my mitochondria stopped making energy. Can I drink coffee with sugar added?"

The employee states, "That will be $3.00,".

"Can I pay for my protein?"

"Why Yes," asks an employee.

The cell commands the ribosome to produce three proteins. In reality, the ribosome produces five proteins.

The cell is asking "What can I do with these extra two proteins?"

"Mr. Lysosome says, "I'll take these. I will break down old waste,"

Mr. Cell is paid with new protein and drinks coffee.

Spending a little more time to create stories, they can make it easier to remember the details later. Making a sentence or story can be entertaining and powerful as stories are generally more easy to remember. The stories transform written text into images that force the brain to build additional neural pathways that connect to the information.These additional pathways assist your brain find the information later.

Technique #4: Focus, Hook, Recall

To help you remember new information, make it a habit of performing this three-step process.

1. Remove any factors that impede your focus. The biggest enemies of focus are distractions that are distracting your attention. Make sure to reduce the information that you're studying to fundamental details. Be sure to consider how the subject is interconnected and builds on the other material.

2. "HOOK "HOOK" could be a simple technique to aid your brain retain information more easily. For instance, when you learn names, a hook will be a way of identifying the name with a particular feature. For instance, a girl called Sandy wearing brown hair lets you associate the name with hair color. To "hook" your data you can use techniques like pictures, visualization songs, sentences graphic organizers or any other method that you employ to aid your brain in organizing new information.

3. Then, you can test your memory with active recall. This could include making mini quizzes, explaining to someone else about the latest information, or responding to questions on the new material.

Notecards are a great way to store your notes and then review them frequently. The great thing about notecards is that they're simple to carry around.

Additionally, when you write notes your brain is learning the subject. The addition of illustrations and pictures to your notecards can help you to learn.

Technique #5: Linking Ideas

You can make your list by connecting the ideas with a narrative in which one event is linked to another. Let's say you've got this list of items:

The Keys Watch, the wallet passport Bug spray

Red cars are the source of information.

You head to your car in red and you put your keys in the door. There is a clown asking to see your purse. The clown is wearing a an enormous watch on their wrist, and an ID card inside their shirt pocket. You quickly think of spraying the clown with insect spray.

You can learn about the states and countries by writing an account

For instance, Georgia, Maine, Tennessee, Utah, and Michigan

Georgia is George Washington

Maine = man

Tennessee= Ten

Utah = unicycle

Michigan is Mimi (my grandma's maiden name)

Then, you write the same story as you did prior to, using an anchor and every event connected to one another.

Anchor = pool

When you're at the pool, are able to see George Washington in a bathing suit talking to a man who has 10 heads on a bicycle and Mimi serves the cupcakes.

Technique #6: Body Stations

Make use of your body as a prop to aid in memorizing lists and facts or other key details.

Here's the way it is done:

You'll be able to remember through 10 different areas in your body. Beginning from high up on your head, and moving towards the bottom.

Your head's top and your eyes, ears, your nose and finally your teeth. your shoulder, your throat the collarbone, the stomach and then the seat (buttocks).

Then, you'll imagine each item, or object you have selected from your list in every one of your body stations.

I will present a short example. I will then memorize the states that begin by the letters A, in alphabetical order. These include Alabama, Alaska, Arizona,Arkansas

Alabama is known for its football, so I put the ball on my head. I wear goggles over my eyes to shield myself from Alaska snow. I apply sunscreen on my nose to block sunburn in the Arizona sunlight, enjoy listening to Bill Clinton speak in Arkansas.

The stories and images aid in the retention of information and help with long lists.

Technique #7: Memory Palace

This method of memory has been utilized for a long time by memory experts. It's like the use of your own body for remembering objects, however instead of using your body, you make use of different objects and rooms within each room as visual props that help remember objects. You can continue adding more rooms or props to your memory palace.

I'll use the four states as an illustration. My house is my castle. Inside my kitchen I make use of the fridge, bar television, lamp, and bar.

I'll imagine an Alabama football in the bar in Alabama The refrigerator has been chilly for Alabama and the lamp is shining as if it's Arizona while Bill Clinton is speaking on the television.

Summary Highlights

Utilize memory strategies to recall key information such as lists, locations and other items that you must remember. Utilizing these methods is more efficient than memorization by rote, but it is also enjoyable, and permits you to be more creative while you're learning.

Seven memory techniques include:

* Journey Method
* Mind Map
* Story or Sentence
* Hook, Focus Recall
* Linking Ideas
* Body Stations
* Memory Palace

Chapter 16: The Quick Study Strategies

The main issue for pupils is they do not have strategies for studying. They just fumble on notes and books and do not know the proper method of studying.

Learning involves the proper implementation of strategies, and the correct mental attitude. You can't just read books and hope to get enough knowledge or recall the information you've read.

Recalling and reading are two distinct processes. However, your ability to recall the information you've read is dependent on your reading style. In this case, many students have trouble at school because they do not use the correct strategy for reading.

In this section I will discuss some of the more effective strategies that you can employ to achieve your academic objectives.

Let's begin.

5 Strategies to Hold More Information while reading the Book

The main benefit that you can get from being in school is that you're inundated with knowledge that you can apply in your daily life. Schools teach students to take their time reading and learning all they can. But, remembering a huge amount of information in books can be an issue for many students. This is because they lack an effective method of reading. They pick up their books or notes and then read. It's not the best way to learn. It's enjoyable, but not productive.

Many students do not comprehend the reason for why they even read books in the first in the first. Most people believe that reading is only required to pass an test. There are only a few students truly view reading as a way of getting ready for their career.

However, whatever purpose you might be serving, the main problem is remembering important details. We all struggle to recall what we've read. It happens every day, but particularly for students. That's that I have created this section in the book to provide you with tips to help you make the most of your time reading your books.

The following are the basic principles to a successful reading. To be able to remember more of the information you have read, you must...

1. Determine your goal

To make sure you retain the information while studying or reading, it is important to have a goal. Before you even open your book or take a note, ask yourself what you are looking for in it. What's the purpose behind it? Your motive should be in line with your goals.

The book you read without having a purpose in mind is not worth reading. It's like digging for gold without keeping it in a vault. This way you're wasting effort and time.

Many students are exactly like this. They study their books without any desire to study. Therefore, when the tests come they have to struggle. They didn't realize how important learning to learn is far more crucial than reading. It doesn't matter how many books you've have read. The most important thing is how much information you gain from the material you read.

Learning should be the primary motive for reading. As a student the goal in reading is to comprehend the subject matter being covered in class. Reading is the result behaviour that you perform for the sole reason.

Many students are reluctant to read due to the fact that it's boring and boring. They don't like reading, and often have to read. In the end, they fail on their exams.

If you're looking to learn more from the books you read, you have to enjoy the process. You must enjoy reading. You should enjoy the possibility of learning the wealth of knowledge instead of hating it. Since if you keep pushing away from the learning course, your life at school is going to be stressful and unpleasant.

The students who succeed in their academic endeavours typically not because they're good at what they do, but because they are passionate about it. They are driven by the work they do.

I remember vividly my first experience when I went to the university , where I earned my masters degree from AB Psychology. It wasn't my goal to enroll in the course. What I wanted to take for was in the BS Accountancy course. But due to a few reasons (a long story I won't be able to tell you in this book with completeness) the school would not let me take the course. Thus, I was accepted into my AB Psychology program.

As passing years went by I began to fall in love with psychology. Actually, I won many of the top academic prizes that students want to attain. The majority of my successes to my love for what I do. I'm passionate about my work even when it wasn't my first choice.

The most important thing that I discovered from my experience is that you will be more effective at what you do when you are passionate about doing it with passion. In other words, you'll gain more knowledge from studying by putting your whole heart into it. In the end, I discovered it is a passion you can nurture within yourself. If you've got an underlying purpose then it won't be difficult to fall in love with the things you've avoided doing prior to.

2. Teacher

The light of knowledge is. However, just having a light not enough. It must be used. The best way to make use of it is to share it with others. Sharing information is what gives it its worth it. Imagine the scenario if Albert Einstein did not share his discoveries about relativity? The world may not be aware the fact that space and time are the governing factors in our lives.

The most satisfying method to share your knowledge is to impart the same to other people. Imagine yourself as a teacher. Discuss what you have learned with your friends, classmates and loved ones.

Being able to share is one of the things that make my work (as an educator) more significant. The greatest aspect of being an educator is that I learn subjects that will later help my students. Teachers help students satisfy their thirst for knowledge and hunger. And , the best is that the students will cherish it for the rest of their lives (well they might, but not all students will be able to cherish it for a lifetime).

The best thing about sharing what you've learned in school is the fact that you'll be able to see how well you know the subject matter you're discussing.

As an undergraduate, I was the first one to go through the lesson long before the tests. That's why the majority of my classmates would ask me to help them comprehend the subject matter we discussed in class. Therefore, I was there whenever I could.

What I realized was the fact that teaching not just help them comprehend but also allowed me to assess whether I really comprehended the subject. If I was able to explain it in a very clear way it is a sign that I knew the subject. If not, I'd have to revisit my notebooks and books and go through them again. What I learned by sharing my knowledge, I gained many advantages.

3. Highlight important points

As a student I was not a fan of marking my notes or books. It made my notes look ugly and messy. But as I prepared to pass my board exam I realized that creating some highlights is useful and beneficial.

The act of highlighting important points makes it easier for you to find important details. Marking your books or notes will aid you in finding crucial information within the page. Therefore, next time you'll not have to spend time searching for the crucial information you need.

After having read a book, place it back on the shelf for several days. You can then read it over. If you can remember why you highlighted certain parts of it (the details connected to it) it means you've absorbed the information. You've acquired new skills or knowledge.

4. Your imagination can be a great help greatly

To make sure you retain more information when reading, create a mental image of the information you have read. Our brains love visuals. The brain stores much more information from visuals than text.

If you are reading an article Try to make an image of the text. Convert that information into images. This makes the process of learning more enjoyable. Why? Because the brain associates information with things that are related to that information.

Let me give you an example. Let's say you head into your room to grab something (probably an item like a pen) and the moment you arrive, you forget the reason for your visit. Instead of trying to recall it, simply return to where you were (probably at the table) and you'll be able to remember it. Why? Because you observe things related to the pen you thought of as a pen.

It's the way our brain functions. It's called association.

5. Use your brain's tricks to get you to take breaks

Information overload diminishes your brain capacity. "The higher the volume of data you consume the less you think and the more disjointed the brain's system is."

How do we stop overloaded information? Simple, stop for five minutes. Take down your notebook, your book you're reading or even the gadget(s). Going to the bathroom could be beneficial in reviving your mind. "A short break in the brain is one method you can keep your brain's power on the highest level."

6. Your brain can trick you into slowing down

Learning a lot of things in a short amount of time is inefficient. Why? Our brains can't take in rapid information. This is that cramming your notes at night prior to the test is not efficient. Instead of absorbing all your notes at once you should concentrate only on one part and one chapter at each chapter. Pick a subject and concentrate on it and you'll become a more effective learner.

7. Use what you've learned

I have heard someone say that "Learning isn't an entertainment game." It's the case. Since you can't truly learn if you don't work about it. Also the true meaning of learning is the application.

The greatest benefit of applying information is that it will make you better as a person. Businesses will make more money. Students will do well in their academic pursuits.

A lot of students struggle in school. This is not because they lack the ability to think, but because they are doing it in a incorrect method. Many students spend their time working in an unproductive manner. This includes you. What is wrong? There are more effective ways to learn your subject.

They are also tested and proven scientifically.

Generation X students have a wealth of resources available to utilize. However, they do it in a way that isn't optimal. If you're looking to be successful in school, it is essential use these strategies or other strategies that have been tested and proven scientifically effective to increase your potential as an student.

Chapter 17: Preparing for Classes

Get Organized

Many people say they don't have time to be organized. This is an absurd claim, and the reason is that A well-organized system saves time. It can save you a lot of time. It's more than just possessing a beautiful notebook and your papers are hole punched. The proper organization addresses both the tangible and intangible.

Finding the right information is essential and you should spend a bit of your time prior to classes even begin to become physically organized. Make sure you have notebooks, binders and folders, or whatever else will help you find important information quickly.

Each term I mark folders with an organizer that closes (so there is no chance of a leak) and then I put my papers in the proper places as I receive them. I never lose any papers because of this.

There are two distinct pockets that are for homework and homework. Anything I must do or need to submit goes in there. I don't forget to complete or return assignments because of this. The first thing to keep inside my binder weekly calendar. I design them each period. They can also be used as a schedule.

General Chemistry 3 - MWF (10:15-11:20)			
Chemistry 3 Lab - T (2:30-5:20)			
Organic Chemistry - TR (8:00-9:50)			
Organic Chemistry Lab - M (1:00-4:50)			
Notes			

I record each homework assignment, each reminder, and any other information that I could require when the teacher has it. If I find anything I didn't cross off at the time the week is over I then rewrite it on the each week's homework sheets. Sometimes, I'll have to rewrite something each week throughout the course. For instance I was in a Shakespeare class I took, we were given the essay's final guidelines in the very first class day. I took note of it and then continued to write it each week until I completed the essay (which was the last week of class because I had a tendency to procrastinate frequently). Because I recorded it often, I didn't forget that it was due to be completed. I also considered the essay in every class since I noticed it on my homework sheets and this led me to note down the specific information from the class that I planned to include in the final paper. When I finally got around to writing it, I had the majority of it laid out in my head. All I had to do was write.

If you can take just ten minutes at the conclusion of each week to examine your order and correct anything not in place You'll reduce time in the end. If you perform a quick inspection at the beginning and/or at the end of each class it will become a habit and I'm betting you'll not need to devote 10 minutes at the end each week.

The intangible management of time may be more crucial than physical organization, however paradoxically, only when one is physically organized. If I'm really attracted to a specific homework project or reading assignment I shouldn't be spending more than two hours at work before taking to take a break. So, I'm given 120 minutes to complete my work accomplished before having to complete something different. If I have to spend 45 minutes searching for documents or checking my email or glancing off into space or trying to remove the stain that's never bothered me from the shirt I don't wear...I will lose a substantial portion of my time at work that is quality. The best way to combat this issue and increase the amount of my 120 minutes that I am productive is...organization! Take five or ten minutes prior to the beginning of your working day to write a to-do list, or a sketch of what you'll do over the next 60-120 (or greater) minutes. When you feel disoriented, lost in thought or confused about what you should do, take a look at your list of tasks and start working on what you think is most important. If it takes you ten minutes to reduce your working time it's only necessary to save the time of ten minutes to be worth it. I'm sure you'll be able to save more than ten mins simply by moving to the next thing that you have to complete instead of having to stop your work to think about your next move.

Another aspect to consider in time management is how you'll be able to finish everything. I am a fan of the weekly sheets of my planner to help with this. Each time I add something to my planner I think about putting aside 125 percent of the time that I believe the task is going to take at the very least to complete it. When I organize everything in this way even if I fail to adhere to the plan (which I seldom do) I notice that I've got more time during the week than I expected which helps keep my stress at bay. In addition, I notice less stress when I complete an assignment in a shorter time than I planned.

Find a teacher who you can Learn from In a Good Way

There are only two possible reasons I've failed in the classroom. 1.) I didn't spend enough time studying the subject 2.) I had a teacher who I found to be horrible. Let's concentrate on the second issue the teachers. We must admit that not every teacher is capable of teaching well. There are many reasons why teachers don't do a good job of teaching. Some are rigid and are able to only present information in one manner and that's not enough. Many are too detailed and will not be able to pass due to omitted commas or mistakes in spelling when the reasoning behind your essay is perfect and even genius. There are many reasons why teachers are poor. There is nothing you can do to make a difference to a teacher you don't like (though there are methods to make it work in a class taught by an unprofessional teacher) however, you are able to in a way pick your teachers. If there are two teachers teaching the class you'd like to enroll in, locate both and ask them to answer a few questions on the subject they'll be teaching. Only a few minutes of discussion talking to a teacher can be enough to save you a whole week of stress.

I do this. I research which teachers are teaching each term, and then locate their office phone number or email address, and then schedule an appointment with them. I'll also look them up on www.RateMyProfessors.com, though I find the in person meetings to be WAY more helpful.

Teachers' personal time has another, more difficult to appreciate benefit: once you establish a rapport with the teacher, it's more easy to learn from their teaching methods. Take a look at that: have you and your favorite friend ever spoken a word that was clear to anyone else than you? You got them to believe because you are familiar with the person they are. You're aware of their thinking process. Teachers are human beings as you are your best friend. you can discover the way they think. If you can better understand their personality and the more comfortable it will be to understand the lessons they impart. It's also easier to focus on those you admire, love or admire. There was a teacher in my high school that I couldn't be around. The class was always a battle. Then one day I had to complain about her to a different teacher and my view changed. The teacher I liked, shared with me about the life of the teacher I didn't like. She was a world traveler and had studied in a vast range of fascinating places, and met amazing people. She is fluent in five languages. She truly is an amazing intelligent, competent human being. Although I did not like her style of teaching I admired her and increased over time. I was more attracted to the things she said and eventually learned lots of information about writing and history from her.

I have made it a priority to know about my teachers as early as possible during the term. The sooner I get to get to know them and get to know them, the more fun I can have in class. I am always asking questions in class and come back after class to answer the same questions, I laugh with my teacher, and I provide interesting articles to students that relate to the class or specialization and ask them to do the exact same. If you build an enthralling relationship between teacher and students and you have an excellent experience in your classroom. College is a place of community, learn to get to know the people who lead your neighborhood.

Sometimes, building a positive student-teacher relationship can be impossible.This is only an issue when you have a poor teacher. In these instances, there are a couple of options. You can either drop the class, or find another method to earn the credits you require. I would suggest that you stop this option as a last resort. Better to follow all of the above.

1.) Find someone on the internet who teaches the same content. There are a myriad of websites that teach every aspect you could think of. There is an online video that can help make your life simpler. If you can get the necessary information from a different teacher and then use it in an instructor who you don't like, you'll be more successful.

The list of sites is available within the annexe.

2.) talk to other students, to the teacher, and colleagues. If you're experiencing problems with a teacher, the chances that other students are having issues also. In either case, or in an entire group, record exactly what your teacher does or does not do that makes it difficult to learn. Talk about these issues with your teacher in a non-discriminatory way. The majority of teachers are willing to changing how they teach, if they know how to modify the method. If a teacher isn't willing or does not see any change then ask a member of the faculty to join an appointment with your teacher and assist to resolve the issue.

Select Your Classes Be Careful

If I say you should pick your classes with care, I am referring to two things. First, choose classes you are interested in to ensure that you're more motivated to finish the assignment. This is a tiny tip that could have significant implications. Pick a subject that interests you. Choose something you are truly interested to study. If you're not quite sure what interests you, go through the descriptions for as many courses you can. Research those you are most interested in and then select those that you think are the most interesting. Try a variety of classes until you discover something you're excited to study. If you're not happy studying a subject at college, you're probably not going to like a job associated with the subject in the future.

Then, create the most efficient schedule that you can. Personally, I try to avoid early morning commitments and attempt to schedule at least one hour that is free between classes when I'm at the campus with nothing else to do but work. Also, I try my best to not have to hurry. For instance, I don't have two classes on different campuses back to back. I'd rather chat with the instructor for a couple of minutes after class, and then take a stroll around to get my mind clear before arriving at class at a couple of minutes earlier look over the syllabus to know the agenda of the class, go over my homework, take water to drink and eat a meal, or whatever else can help me get through my next job.

There's there is only so much that you are able to accomplish. Sometimes, you are stuck with a bad schedule, or with a bad teacher. I'm writing about it because each period I've taken the extra time working on my schedule. I congratulate myself over and over again for it. Consider it in this way: If you're spending five hours doing your schedule then you'll only need to spare yourself five hours of stress later to make it worth it. If your schedule is 10 weeks long, that's six minutes of work per day. With a busy schedule and a headache that lasts for six minutes each day isn't many.

Chapter 18: Manage your time effectively

Related to the previous factors is the subject of managing time. Making a time planner, according to section 1 is essential, however this isn't all there is to time management. There are many other factors you must keep in mind when you want to be an efficient time manager.

It's vital to be aware of the times when you are at your most alert. These are times when your brain is the most active and working at its best. At your highest mental levels you'll be able to easily comprehend things that you struggle to comprehend and even ask why it was once difficult. You can use your mental peak times to tackle those subjects that normally are difficult for you, which will allow you to cut down on time. If you normally struggle to grasp some Physics concepts in as little as 2 hours, it should not be a surprise to find that in your chosen times that the same concepts will be fully understood in less than one hour, thus saving you the remaining time. Utilizing your best mental hours for subjects that are easy would be wasteful of your time. If that your peak hour is midnight, then go to bed early, and set your alarm to about 15 minutes prior to midnight. Then go to the study room as hard as you can.

Knowing your peak mental capacity is crucial as is knowing your sleep time. Doing your best to keep yourself awake when to fall asleep could be a waste of time. It is possible that you will spend all day recovering from a quick nap, that you never be unable to do anything worthwhile doing it. Make the most of your rest when you are ready to go to bed.

Procrastination is an issue you need to tackle unflinchingly when trying to organize your time. There are certain disciplines in which they suggest that you put off activities in the hope that the delay will allow you to have a clearer mind. It might work in these areas but not in the realm of studying. Instead of looking for reasons to put off studying, look for reasons not to delay and you won't regret it. Take care of all the things that cause you to delay your studies. Do not let the distraction of chatting with your friend distract you from something as vital and vital as studying. You could do it at any time. Be especially cautious of procrastination that looks like it's not because the impact on your study is exactly the similar.

Effectively managing your time requires planning time for rest breaks. As if you study the same subject every hour doesn't yield the results you want, committing to studying all day long without taking breaks can result in the exact same. Have a break where you're not doing anything. Chat with your buddies, as long as you don't intend to consume your next time period of study and cause you to delay your studies. It is possible to take a short walk, take a break, eat a meal or drink a glass of juice. Most times, as you do this, you'll notice your brain is digesting what you've been studying, without intentional effort by you.

It is also beneficial to not hesitate to break for a moment if you're looking for it. So, whenever you are in the mood to take that break, make sure you take. This can help you prevent lapses in concentration, that happen when all you have to do is look at the time at 5 seconds every time to determine whether it's enough time to break. It is a guarantee that once you're in a state of mind, anything you try to learn will be lost.

Get organized

Organization is an essential component of the research process which is the reason it cannot be treated as a separate thing even though it is an essential aspect of planning since a sloppy plan isn't a plan all the time. There is many interconnections between planning and organization.

Being organized when doing what you wish to accomplish allows you to take deliberate actions. The most important thing to be planned is the choice of study time. It is not enough to pick any study time, however, you must choose an exact time due to the benefits it can bring you. It is possible to choose to study immediately following a lecture to ensure maximum retention of what might have learned in the lecture. Or, you may want to take your time studying prior to the lecture so you can comprehend exactly what your lecturer talking about more clearly. What are the benefits to you studying at a specific duration?

Selecting the best subjects to study at certain time periods is another aspect organizing. Make sure that the subjects are organized so that you have some space between subjects that share similar material. If, for instance, you want to take classes in Economics as well as Business Studies, it would be a mistake to take one course before the other. There is a lot of overlap in these fields that could cause confusion and cause confusion and confusion facts. It is therefore recommended to place a separate subject in between to avoid any interference.

Another strategy that you could employ is to arrange your studies in a manner that over time, you develop the habit of studying or a ritual. You can accomplish this by setting a specific period of time to focus on a specific topic. For instance, you could decide to do Math every day at 2pm. It is a habit that you can adhere to without breaking the chain for a certain period of time, and eventually a pattern will begin to emerge where your brain is geared to Math when 2 pm is close. This is a way of conserving time over the long term as you don't have to force your brain into an area of study when you're ready to tackle it.

It is possible to take this further by having different spaces or rooms to accommodate various subjects. This will force your brain to adapting to the environment. It is possible that your mind will change to an accounting mood once you enter the Accounting setting, which will grant you the precious minutes. If you're writing notes, highlighters can be used to highlight specific areas. the more effective if you select a particular colour for a certain topic so that your brain will be able to associate the highlighter of lemon with French or French-inspired, for instance.

Conclusion

Knowledge and intelligence is a way of living and not a characteristic. There are many different motives for the reasons why people seek the pursuit of intelligence, ultimately it'll depend on the way you treat yourself and the value you place on your own thoughts which will show up.

I hope that you discovered this book to be helpful, now that you are provided with the necessary knowledge, now is the time to put into practice the methods taught and elevate your life to the next level.

I hope that you enjoyed reading this book the same way I enjoyed writing it.

www.ingramcontent.com/pod-product-compliance
Lightning Source LLC
Chambersburg PA
CBHW071839080526
44589CB00012B/1051